616.863
C678d
2

THE DRUG
DILEMMA

McGRAW-HILL SERIES IN HEALTH EDUCATION

Deobold B. Van Dalen, Consulting Editor

Cohen: The Drug Dilemma

Dalrymple: Sex Is for Real: Human Sexuality and Sexual Responsibility

Diehl: Tobacco and Your Health: The Smoking Controversy

Fort: Alcohol: Our Biggest Drug Problem

Martin: Mental Health/Mental Illness: Revolution in Progress

Ross and O'Rourke: Understanding the Heart and Its Diseases

THE DRUG DILEMMA

Second Edition ✓

Sidney Cohen, M.D.

Clinical Professor of Psychiatry, U.C.L.A.
Former Director, Division of
Narcotic Addiction and Drug Abuse,
National Institute of Mental Health,
Washington, D.C.

McGraw-Hill Book Company

New York St. Louis San Francisco Auckland
Düsseldorf Johannesburg Kuala Lumpur London
Mexico Montreal New Delhi Panama Paris
São Paulo Singapore Sydney Tokyo Toronto

The Drug Dilemma

Copyright © 1969, 1976 by McGraw-Hill, Inc. All rights reserved.
Printed in the United States of America. No part of this publication
may be reproduced, stored in a retrieval system, or transmitted, in any
form or by any means, electronic, mechanical, photocopying, recording, or
otherwise, without the prior written permission of the publisher.

1234567890BPBP798765

This book was set in Press Roman by Allen Wayne Technical Corp.
The editor was Richard R. Wright;
the designer was Allen Wayne Technical Corp.;
the production supervisor was Judi Allen.
The cover was designed by Irving Freeman.
The Book Press, Inc., was printer and binder.

Library of Congress Cataloging in Publication Data

Cohen, Sidney, date
  The drug dilemma.

  Bibliography: p.
  1. Narcotic habit—United States. 2. Drug
abuse—United States. I. Title. [DNLM: 1. Drug
abuse. 2. Drug addiction. WM270 C678d]
HV5825.C6 1976   616.8'63   75-12901
ISBN 0-07-011587-7
ISBN 0-07-011588-5 pbk.

To ILSE, DOROTHY, and RICHARD

35263

Contents

Preface to the Second Edition ix

Preface to the First Edition xi

Introduction xiii

Chapter 1 "Those Who Will Not Learn from History..." 1

Chapter 2 Some Definitions 6

Chapter 3 The Psychedelics ... LSD and Others 10

Chapter 4 The Psychedelics ... Marihuana 22

Chapter 5 Amphetamines, Cocaine, and Other Stimulants 31

Chapter 6 The Narcotics 38

Chapter 7 The Sedatives and Tranquilizers 51

Chapter 8 The Volatile Solvents and Other Anesthetics 56

Chapter 9 Alcohol, a Dangerous Drug 59

Chapter 10 Deliriants, Old and New 68

Chapter 11 The "Head" 72

Chapter 12 The Drug Dilemmas 79

Summary of Drug Effects 90

Additional Reading 93

Glossary of Drug Slang 98

Preface
to the Second Edition

This second edition is almost a new book. Much of it has been re-written, and two new chapters have been added. These revisions have become necessary because the drug scene changes, new treatments emerge, and research brings forth new information. The rapidity of change in the dependency disorders makes obsolete that which was written only a few years ago.

We are entering a new phase of the national drug problem. Five years ago when the first edition was written, the nonmedical use of mind-altering drugs was expanding incredibly. Prevention and re-habilitation services were fragmentary. The general public considered drug addiction the nation's second major problem. Now we have entered a more stable phase in which destructive drug use remains high, but the panicky response has waned. Just as it was unwise to overreact to the situation when it flared up, it would be unwise to believe that we have somehow resolved the problem. If our best efforts do not continue, new outbreaks can swing the prevalence curve up-ward again. An epidemic is not over when reports of new cases begin to decrease. Only when the foci of infection are brought under con-trol can we begin to feel complacent. For the drug abuse problem, that time is not predictable.

Sidney Cohen

Preface
to the First Edition

The Drug Dilemma was designed for those who teach and counsel students. Since parents are intimately involved in their children's learning in important life situations and over prolonged periods, they may find relevant information about drug misuse here. But the book was not designed to exclude the student himself. Indeed, he or she is the ultimate consumer, whether it be directly by reading or indirectly by class or group discussion.

Obviously, young men and women have widely varying amounts of information about the mind-altering drugs. For that reason many levels of discussion are included, from the historical and physiological to the psychological and philosophic. It is hoped that most of the questions that arise have been answered, even when that answer can only be, "We don't know today." In fact, much of the book's material has been developed from questions asked by high school, college, and graduate students, by student health service personnel, and by deans of students.

Mind-altering drugs occupy a prominent place in the interests of students today. From the number of letters I received requesting information, they must be first in popularity as a subject for English themes, science reports, and term papers. This curiosity is healthy, and we can only hope that factual material is available for students' consideration. It is not easy for the mass news media to be accurate without overemphasizing the novel and the sensational. Neither can we expect that those whose positions have polarized at one extreme or another will be reliably factual. No one is without some bias; I hope that mine has not distorted the information offered here.

Sidney Cohen

Introduction

In a world undergoing enormous changes, where familial and social supports are eroding, and established beliefs are gradually being demolished, it is natural that many will try to modify their awareness—to ease the uncertainties of the day, to avoid psychic pain, to somehow achieve pleasure, to find faith. The old gods falter; the old goals seem pointless. What is left but to chemically dull the senses or, alternatively, create new illusions, new utopian worlds? So it has been in every period of stress; so it is today.

Man changes his world enormously but himself minimally. He has created instant news, transportation that arrives before it has departed, and vast power from imploded atoms; but he remains the superb technological master concealing the impulsive, frightened child within. The training of his intellect has far exceeded the training of his emotions. His rational cerebral cortex outstrips his emotional midbrain.

This disparity between our emotional immaturity and the uncertainties of burgeoning power makes for a threatening and precarious predicament: We try to train ourselves and our children in emotional growth and discipline, and we attempt to reduce cruelty, correct injustice, counteract intolerance, prevent dehumanization, and protest against the mindless exploitation of nature. Others take another route: Their nerve fails, hopelessness prevails, and they proceed to withdraw from the grinding frustrations. They egotistically seek the pleasures and demand the freedoms of the human encounter but refuse its responsibilities. This all can be done without drugs; with drugs it is so much easier.

These are only some of the reasons for the current upsurge of drug-taking behavior among the young in mind. The avoidance of life stress, the retreat from problem solving, the refusal to cope with adversity, the surrender to defeat, the quest for relevance, and "the death of God"—these and other perplexing situations call forth a search for pharmacological release.

Many of us suffer from a serious disease of affluence: direction-lessness. No longer need large segments of this society focus on the struggle to avoid hunger, thirst, and the extremes of temperature that preoccupied their fathers. Unfortunately, new directions and new goals have not yet been acquired. Meanwhile for others the crushing diseases of poverty remain, and these enhance escape in the form of a bedrugged existence. Although we cannot agree with the the means, we can try to understand the attractiveness of oblivion, the distancing from hurt, or the fabulous fantasies that drugs can bring.

It is my belief that when a person becomes a "head,"—be it "pothead," "hophead," "acidhead," "pillhead," or "rumhead"—he has relinquished a core aspect of his existence. He has surrendered his human freedom, his individuation—the potion has become the master. Tillich would have said that his personal "centeredness" has been lost. To paraphrase the statement made about the person vulnerable to alcohol: First the person takes the drug, then the drug takes the person.

Naturally, as with drink, many kinds of drug users exist. But the illegality and the culture-alien aspects of drug usage make it more socially hazardous than the misuse of alcohol. Particularly, the bio-logically or psychologically unstable and defeated will become overly involved in excessive taking of mind-altering substances. One is re-minded of the fragment from Edgar Lee Master's *Spoon River Anthology:*

> What is this I hear of sorrow and weariness
> Anger, discontent and dropping hopes?
> Degenerate sons and daughters
> Life is too strong for you
> It takes life to love Life.

"Those Who Will Not Learn from History..."

Contrary to the careless statements one often hears, man is not the only creature that can become dependent upon drugs. Under artificial conditions almost any animal can become addicted, including mice, monkeys, and dogs. Under natural conditions animals tend to avoid intoxicating plants, but horses, cows, and sheep that have grazed on the locoweeds (*Astragulus mollisimus, Oxytropis spendens,* etc.) on the range develop a craving for these weeds. According to Lewin they become an "incurable slave of the passion." One such animal may "turn on" a whole flock by leading them to the locoweed and eating it in their presence. Interestingly, it is the young animal that is especially susceptible to both the intoxicating and debilitating effects of locoweeds.

Man has made strenuous efforts to find mind-altering substances and techniques. The ancient story of fermented honey, grains, and fruits needs no retelling here. Indian hemp and opium have been used for millennia. At times the discovered psychochemical appears to fit many of the needs of the culture. The coca leaf permitted the Andean Indian to work beyond his endurance in the low-oxygen atmosphere 2 miles up. The antifatigue, refreshing effects of the cocaine extracted by chewing a cud of leaves mixed with ashes, sustained them in their bleak struggle for survival. The same alkaloid brought to the cities of Western Europe in the nineteenth century was a disaster to its middle-class users. Availability is a prime consideration. Caapi was found and used by the Amazonian Indians. The iboga bean is gathered for the seething rituals of the Iboga and Oubanghi tribes of what was the French Congo. The Australian aborigines have the leaves of the ener-gizine pituri plant at hand. These they mix with ash and chew whenever they feel let down.

However, easy accessibility to a drug is not always a requirement for its entry into a culture. Pituri trails still can be seen in central Australia over which the aborigines transported the stimulating leaves for hundreds of miles to trade with other tribes. Khat Catha edulis) is a mildly euphoriant plant. It grows in Ethiopia and yet is is fairly universally chewed on the Arabian peninsula. Its transportation from Africa to Asia is a substantial factor in the operating income of the Ethiopian Airlines. The many routes that opium takes to the ultimate consumer of heroin are worldwide. Raw opium is grown in the Far East, the Middle East, and Mexico; it is processed into heroin from Hong Kong to Marseilles; the heroin is delivered to the great ports of the world for distribution down to the lowly "hophead" in the dingy alleys of the larger cities. The profits flow centripetally into the strongboxes of organized crime rings, with the overflow going into numbered bank accounts in Switzerland. Alcohol is displacing some of the more traditional agents for example, kava in Polynesia and the betel nut in the East Indies. Now that rapid transportation has brought an assortment of psychochemicals to the local black marketplace, price and preference, rather than local availability, have become the major factors. The novelty of the drug is very important, as we shall see.

We have gone through cycles of intense drug misuse before. All classes of mind alterers have had their periods of popularity and decline. As one strolls past Needle Park in New York, Haight-Ashbury in San Francisco, or Capsule Corner in Los Angeles. it may appear that a relatively new phenomenon is being observed. This is hardly so. Nor is it necessary to reach back to the bacchanalian orgies of Rome. the

the penny gin of seventeenth-century London, the widespread addiction which attended the opium wars, or the multitudes of Middle Eastern hashish eaters. Just one century ago in the English-speaking countries a flood of drugs was unleashed. It will be instructive to look at that scene briefly so that a more balanced view of our present situation may be achieved.

Just after the Civil War, more distilled spirits were being consumed per capita than today. This occurred despite a vigorous temperance movement. Many of the devout temperance advocates themselves felt no qualms in taking a warming sip of some patent medicine—for example, Hostetter's Bitters, 47 percent alcohol by volume. It is fascinating that no less a psychologist-philosopher than William James wrote in his *Varieties of Religious Experience*, "The sway of alcohol over mankind is unquestionably due to its power to stimulate the mystical faculties of human nature usually crushed to earth by the cold facts and dry criticisms of the sober hour." Our latter-day chemical mystics call alcohol a "downer," and no one even pretends to drink whiskey for its mystical qualities these days.

In England opium usage was really serious during the eighteenth and nineteenth centuries. Rich and poor, poet and peasant, all could buy laudanum (tincture of opium) or gum opium from any apothecary. "Happiness might now be bought for a penny and carried in the waistcoat pocket. Portable ecstasies might be had in a bottle, and peace of mind sent down by the mail," wrote Thomas De Quincey in his *Confessions of an English Opium Eater.* The lyric descriptions of the heavenly mind-releasing effects of opium are strangely reminiscent of the psychedelic narrations of today.

Chloroform and ether were novelties during the nineteenth century. The public was fascinated by these strange, pungent liquids and managed to find ways to misuse them. At Cambridge University chloroform parties were enjoyed for a while, until its toxicity became apparent. The safer ether was more widely used for ether frolics at Harvard and other centers of learning where adventurous young people gathered. These revels took place even before the anesthetic potential of ether was known. But it was not sniffed merely for a cheap drunk. William James, that nineteenth-century arbiter of the religious experience, called it "a stimulator of the mystical consciousness." Ether is now considered a mundane anesthetic; when it first appeared, it was a highly regarded consciousness expander.

Nitrous oxide, commonly called laughing gas, must be adjudged the primary nineteenth-century psychedelic of the English speaking world. Sir Humphry Davy discovered that it could disinhibit in the most delightful and hilarious manner. Many artists and students inhaled it for its voluptuous sensations and entrancing chromatic fantasies. Visions of Paradise, universal truths, and enormous insights were all experienced and duly reported. On college campuses and at certain dinner parties, laughing gas was the fashionable, the only genteel way to become "stoned," to lose one's inhibitions. At sideshows and county fairs nitrous oxide inhalations were dispensed for a quarter. Some customers went on a laughing jag; others discovered final truths. A few met with nothing but a sick stomach and dizziness for their two bits. How interesting that we are beginning to hear about laughing gas abuse again now, a hundred years later.

Unless we learn from it, we are condemned to repeat history. Dismal repetitions of the drug-taking errors of the past are once more under way, with agents much more powerful and diverse and just as incompletely understood. It took thousands of years to recognize the harm that excessive drinking could do for example, that alcohol predisposed to cirrhosis of the liver, brain damage, neuritis, and many deficiency diseases. For centuries opium was not known to be addictive. It was more than 300 years before the carcinogenic potential of tobacco was discovered. Dozens of years had to pass before the Western world recognized cocaine as a dangerous agent. The long latent period that lies between the start of widespread misuse of a drug and the full recognition of its harmful effects is an old story. Of the agents now in vogue, many are known to be harmful, some are claimed to be safe. Regarding the safety of the latter, it may be prudent to consider the old claims of safety for alcohol, opium, tobacco, and cocaine.

It has been said that ours is a drug-taking age. Perhaps we are not entitled to that distinction when we glance back at earlier times. Those who speak of this as an age of drugs seem to justify their misuse on the grounds that others are using antibiotics, tranquilizers, or antidepressants—but in proper amounts and for proper reasons. This is a strange logic. Perhaps this period is better called the age of miracles. Daily we witness the miraculous cures of medicine and the miracles of science and technology. Why should we not expect a miracle pill to cure us of our hurts, provide instant happiness, instant maturity, and instant love?

Many of the drugs which alter consciousness, thought, emotion, and sensation, call them hallucinogenic or psychedelic, have been around for a long time. It is the novelty of each newly touted chemical that makes it singularly attractive. The "psychedelic" state can be obtained by a wide variety of agents in addition to those we ordinarily classify as psychedelic. I have already mentioned anesthetics, narcotics, stimulants, and deliriants that have been called precursors of the mystical experience.

Controls over the abuse of chemicals are necessary, but simply passing laws, however harsh, is rarely a final solution. The abuse of alcohol was not solved by the Volstead Prohibition Act; indeed, the act bred crime and provoked a demoralizing disrespect for the law. More successful, but hardly curative, was the Harrison Narcotics Act, which reduced the number of cocaine and opiate users but created a criminal hierarchy supported by those locked into heroin. The Pure Food and Drug laws successfully swept understandardized, mislabeled, and falsely advertised nostrums from the shelves of the grocer and druggist. Why the varying degrees of success of the three laws? The amount of public support is one part of the answer. Whether the substance is culture-alien or culturally accepted is another. The third part of the answer involves a major task of our day. It is to teach the young how to engage a changing world, and how to establish new goals when the old ones become threadbare and irrelevant.

The lessons of history seem to be: (1) that what appears to be new has happened many times before; (2) that a panicky response to a suddenly apparent social problem like drug abuse is unnecessary and often counterproductive; and (3) that the undesirable new problem can be dealt with by a thoughtful and appropriate response.

We perennially forget the cyclic nature of the development of human beings and of their drug habits. A young person is more curious, less cautious, more impulsive, more willing to take a chance, and certainly more idealistic. Many youths are fascinated by mind-changing drugs, especially the new ones, while their elders are appalled by the dangerous exploration into insufficiently studied chemicals. As the young grow and mature, they tend to withdraw from chemical risk taking. When they become parents, they are dismayed in turn by the goings-on of their adolescents. The generation gap is the distance between the parents' forgetting and their childrens' not knowing.

Chapter 2

Some Definitions

This book will concentrate on the more reasonable concept of drug dependence rather than of habituation or addiction, although these words are not completely abandoned. *Drug dependence* is a state of psychic or physical dependence, or both, arising in a person following administration of a drug on a periodic or continuous basis. But drug dependence is of a highly variable nature, and to be accurate it is necessary to state the kind of dependence. The World Health Organization classifies the following major types of drug dependence:

1 The morphine type
2 The barbiturate-alcohol type
3 The cocaine type
4 The cannabis (marihuana) type
5 The amphetamine type
6 The khat type
7 The hallucinogen (LSD) type

For those who wish to retain the concepts of addiction and habituation, their official definitions are included. Drug addiction is a state caused by periodic or chronic intoxication produced by the repeated consumption of a natural or synthetic drug. Its characteristics include: (1) an overpowering desire or need (compulsion) to continue taking the drug and to obtain it by any means; (2) a tendency to increase the dose (tolerance); (3) the development of physical dependence and an abstinence syndrome on abrupt discontinuance of the drug; and (4) detrimental effects on the individual or on society. Drug habituation is a condition resulting from the repeated consumption of a drug. Its characteristics include: (1) a desire, but not a compulsion, to continue taking the drug for the sense of improved well-being which it engenders; (2) some degree of psychic dependence on the effect of the drug, but absence of physical dependence (and hence of an abstinence syndrome); (3) detrimental effects, if any, primarily on the individual.

Tolerance is the ability of the organism to become used to increasing amounts of the agent upon repetitive exposure. Stated in the opposite manner, the original amount of the drug becomes less effective over time so that larger and larger amounts are needed to provide the original effect. Tolerance develops in many ways; one common mechanism is that the body learns how to destroy the drug more efficiently by the production of larger amounts of the enzyme which metabolizes the drug.

Substances in the same pharmacologic class or in closely related classes demonstrate *cross-tolerance*. If a person has acquired tolerance to alcohol, he ordinarily has some cross-tolerance to other sedatives, tranquilizers, and anesthetics.

Reverse tolerance would be the sensitization of the user to a drug so that less is needed subsequently to produce the initial effect. This term is often used in connection with marihuana. Little evidence exists to indicate that reverse tolerance is a real phenomenon. Instead, the observation that experienced smokers may achieve their preferred state on lesser amounts of the drug can be explained otherwise. Increased efficiency of the smoking process is one possible explanation. Another is the observation that frequent users have learned the altered state of consciousness so well that they identify the earliest effects. When an experienced user is in the company of a smoker he or she may experience a "contact high." In our experiments with marihuana we have found that experienced users often get "high" from smoking placebos (blanks). In experiments where large amounts of marihuana are smoked tolerance rather than reverse tolerance develops.

If an animal or person has become tolerant to a drug, and its use is suddenly discontinued, an *abstinence syndrome* (withdrawal sickness) may appear. The long-term use of the chemical agent has produced a situation in which the body cells have not only adapted to its presence, but their metabolism has so altered that its absence is upsetting. Central nervous system depressants have definite withdrawal symptoms. The stimulants demonstrate a less distinct withdrawal pattern. An excellent example of the abstinence syndrome is the *delirium tremens* (DTs) which begins about 12 to 24 hours after stopping heavy, consistent alcohol or sleeping pill usage. Severe tremulousness, delirium, and convulsions are observed over the next few days. On Skid Row these are referred to as the "shakes," the "horrors," and the "whiskey fits."

Potentiation or *synergism* is the combined effects of two drugs of the same or related classes that result in an impact much greater than that of either drug alone. The use of alcohol and sleeping pills together is synergistic to the point that less than lethal amounts of each may cause death when taken together. *Antagonism* is the neutralization of the effects of one drug by another which acts in an opposite direction. Stimulants are antagonized by sedatives and vice versa. Not all the effects of a drug are antagonized by its antidote. Some drug combinations are taken together to produce a "smoother" effect, e.g., amphetamines and barbiturates or heroin and cocaine.

It is interesting how many pharmacological classes of drugs are capable of abuse. At the depressant end of the scale are *anesthetics* such as ether, alcohol, and laughing gas. They produce relaxation, excitation (as a disinhibiting effect), and finally coma. The pain-assauging *narcotics* include opium and its derivatives—morphine, codeine, and Dilaudid. Heroin is morphine treated with strong acetic acid. Related synthetic preparations like Demerol, methadone, and Percodan are also pain relievers, drive reducers, and sleep inducers. Next in order are *sedatives* like the barbiturates, which quiet, relax, and eventually induce sleep. The *tranquilizers,* for example, Miltown, are sedatives that calm without inducing excessive drowsiness. On the other side of the mood scale are the *stimulants*, which elevate one's mood, alert, and reduce appetite and the need for sleep. They are exemplified by the amphetamines. The *hallucinogens*, or *psychedelics*, are capable of producing perceptual alterations such as illusions and hallucinations intense emotional states, a nonrational. reverie type of thinking, and ego distortions such as loss of self and feelings of complete strangeness. This group is typified by LSD. The *deliriants* induce more mental confusion than the hallucinogens but are just as capable of providing hallucinations, delusions, and changes of emotionality and of the self. Common examples would be belladonna or Jimson weed. Actually, every group mentioned can intoxicate, that is, produce a delirium. It is evident, then, that although many classes of drugs invoke mental changes, the overlap is considerable. Finally, the *convulsants* like picrotoxin and strychnine are a group that produces maximal brain stimulations.

The symptoms of the mind-changing drugs may require defining. *Illusions* are misinterpretations of a sensation e.g. a stain on a wall interpreted as a face. *Hallucinations* are projections onto the environment for which no sensory cue exists, e.g., hearing voices or seeing objects that others are unable to sense. *Delusions* are erroneous beliefs that are not amenable to reason. *Paranoid* refers to incorrect, suspicious, persecutory or grandiose ideas; *paranoia* would be a fixed ideational system preoccupied with a specific erroneous idea. *Mania* includes a flight of ideas, overactivity and distractibility.

Drug abuse itself is worth defining. It is the persistent and usually excessive self-administration of any drug which has resulted in psychological or physical dependence, or which deviates from approved social patterns of the culture. *Polydrug abuse* is the misuse of more than a single agent with all the hazards of potentiation.

Chapter 3

The Psychedelics...
LSD and Others

CLASSIFICATION

A classification of the various psychedelics (also called *hallucinogens*, *psychotomimetics*, *mysticomimetics*, and *psychodysleptics*) may be helpful in understanding their great variety.

1 Those containing an indole nucleus.
   a Lysergic acid diethylamide (LSD, LSD-25, acid) a semisynthetic chemical from the fungus ergot, which grows on spoiled rye grain. Certain other variants of the lysergic acid molecule are hallucinogenic including lysergic acid amide and lysergic acid hydroxyethylamide. These are found in four varieties of tropical American morning glory seeds.
   b Dimethyltryptamine (DMT) in Cohaba snuff, and its analogues.
   c Bufotenine, found with DMT in small quantities in the skin of the toad, *Bufo marines*, the urine of some schizophrenic patients, and possibly in the mushroom *Amanita muscarina* (soma).

   d Psilocybin and psilocin from the *Psilocybe mexicana* mushroom and related varieties.

   e Ibogaine found in the bean and root of the Congolese vine *Tabernanthe iboga.*

   f Harmine and harmeline, contained in South American caapi (also called yage and ayahuasca).

2 Those with a phenthylamine structure

   a Mescaline (3,4,5-trimethoxyphenylethylamine) the active alkaloid of the peyote cactus *Lophophora williamsii.*

   b STP (also DOM), a synthetic compound related to mescaline and amphetamine. Its chemical composition is 2,5-dimethoxy-4-methylamphetamine.

   c MDA (3,4,-methylenedioxyamphetamine) and about 30 other methoxylated amphetamines that are hallucinogenic including TMA and PMA.

3 Miscellaneous structures.

   a THC (Δ-9-tetrahydrocannabinol) the active component from the leaves and flowering tops of marihuana (Indian hemp, *Cannabis sativa*, pot).

   b PCP (phencyclidine, Sernyl, Sernylan, hog, the peace pill), a synthetic veterinary sedative.

   c Ditran (JB-329) is a synthetic, central antichloingenic compound, which acts similarly to the anticholinergics mentioned in 3d.

   d Scopolamine from henbane *Hyocyamus niger*, atropine from the deadly nightshade *Atropa belladonna*, and Jimson weed *Datura strammonium*

LYSERGIC ACID DIETHYLAMIDE (LSD)

It was LSD during the early 1960s that started the current round of drug overuse. Exhorted by "high priest" Timothy Leary and his disciples, the heady talk was of a psychedelic revolution. If we "turned on" with "acid" we would "tune in" on the eternal truths, and then "drop out" of this mad world. The revolution somehow never came about. The devout "acidheads" of that day seem to have greatly reduced or discontinued the use of LSD. Most surveys indicate that LSD is now being used less than a half dozen years ago. It is far from nonexistent, however. Many young people take LSD for a while, but the righteous acidhead is hard to find.

   LSD did not begin with the Leary group. It was synthesized from lysergic acid extracted from ergot by Hofmann in 1938. Hofmann also accidentally discovered its profound psychological properties five years later. During the 20 years following World War II, LSD was intensively studied to unravel the chemistry of the brain, as a experimental treatment of various disorders, including alcoholism, and as a "model psychosis." The latter effort was an interesting, if not quite successful approach. When LSD is taken in a strange, unsupportive setting, a psychosis with delusional thinking, anxiety, hallucinations, and loss of the ability to differentiate internal from external sensations may occur. In later years this state was called a "bum trip," but originally it was a model psychosis. The hope was that the ability to produce madness in a laboratory could lead to breakthroughs in the study of schizophrenia. Although much was learned, the present feeling is that the LSD psychosis does not mimic the schizophrenic psychosis as well as other agents such as the high-dose amphetamine state.

Physiological Effects and Side Effects

LSD is one of the most powerful drugs known. As little as 20 mcg (micrograms) will produce an effect in most people. There are over a million 20-mcg doses in an ounce. The average dose is 100 mcg. When this amount is swallowed nothing is noticed for 20 to 120 minutes; then the symptoms increase to a peak 2 to 4 hours after ingestion. Thereafter, the drug's activity wanes, and in 8 to 12 hours recovery is usually complete. Larger amounts up to 1,000 mcg have been taken, producing considerable intensification and prolongation of the experience. The lethal dose for human beings is calculated at 15,000 mcg.

It should be remembered that street LSD is a highly variable material. It may be almost pure LSD, but PCP, amphetamines, strychnine, and unidentifiable substances have sometimes been found. The dosage is ordinarily overstated by a wide margin, but it is occasionally underestimated.

Tolerance develops rapidly. If the same dose is taken for a few days little will be noted by the fourth day. Tolerance is also rapidly lost, usually within 48 hours. Cross-tolerance to mescaline and psilocybin occurs, indicating that they probably act on similar neurochemical systems. Withdrawal symptoms do not appear even when LSD has been used consistently; therefore, the drug cannot be called physically addictive. Psychological dependence is known in some people. Stimulants and other hallucinogens potentiate LSD activity; sedatives and tranquilizers antagonize it. LSD can now be detected in body fluids, but the test is not yet commercially available.

The single most notable physical sign of LSD is dilation of the pupils. Nausea, more rarely vomiting, chilliness, flushing, and shakiness are sometimes observed. Blood pressure, body temperature, and heart rate tend to rise slightly. Side effects are very infrequent. In very rare instances, cardiac collapse or a major convulsion have been reported. Death directly due to LSD poisoning is not known.

The question of chromosomal damage can now be summarized with a fair degree of confidence. Pure LSD in average amounts does not appear to produce changes in chromosomal structure. Very large amounts can act as a mild mutagen. The earlier reports of breakage of chromosomes apparently were due less to LSD than to the taking of a wide variety of other drugs, viral infections, malnutrition, and other aspects of the street way of life. Taking LSD during the first three months of pregnancy would be very imprudent as is true of many other chemicals. An increased incidence of abortions has been recorded in women who have used the drug during the first trimester.

Whether LSD causes brain damage is another issue that is often raised. It appears that some persistent users may sustain recent memory defects, vagueness, confusion, and some disorientation for a time after their last trip. These same symptoms are noted in people who have sustained brain damage due to aging or trauma. When a brain disturbance is associated with LSD, it is often reversible over time; only a few people remain blunted and disorganized due to chronic LSD usage.

Psychological Effects and Side Effects

It is not easy to describe the LSD state because it is so variable and essentially nonverbal. Furthermore, the pharmacological action of the drug is but one of many factors that determine the nature of the experience. Other factors include the setting, the set, or expectations, the personality and mood of the subject, the impact of those in contact with the subjects, their knowledge of the drug effects, and other variables.

One of the earliest signs are a lightening of the grey field we ordinarily see with our eyes closed. Then, a colorful pattern of geometric designs may move across the visual field. Later, these may become complex images, people, places, or objects. With open eyes, viewed objects are more intense and colorful. The afterimage of moving objects is prolonged. Stationary objects may appear to move or breathe, and other illusions may be seen. Visual hallucinations seeing things that are not there are rather infrequent. Colors may be heard or the "scent of music" described. These synesthesias, or crossing over of sensory stimuli, are another intriguing aspect of the experience. Often the subject states that what is looked at has a great significance, beauty, and meaning. Hearing can be intensified with background sounds intruding into awareness. Some people find music unusually enchanting. Taste, smell, and touch are similarly sensitized. The sense of time is usually enormously slowed so that the experience seems to go on forever.

The feeling-tone is generally one of euphoria, even ecstasy. Thinking is fantasy-laden and reverie-like, and with high doses logical thinking does not exist. The "me" may dissolve, and the idea of one's body may be completely altered.

Awareness of the fact that a drug has been taken to account for the strange state is almost always preserved. In fact, subjects can pull themselves together and come back to normal if necessary, and then slip back as they let go again.

It is clear that if these striking mental changes develop in the context of fear or mistrust, a very negative reaction will occur. About 10 percent of LSD experiences are panicky and frightening. These are the "bummers" or "freakouts." Horrifying experiences can result from the firm belief that one will never recover, but will remain insane or die. They also occur if personal repressed memories are recalled which are too overwhelming to be dealt with or suppressed. Chaotic surroundings, lack of support, and ambiguous communications are further causes of bad trips. The side effects that will be described are more likely to follow a bummer than a positive experience.

During the period of LSD intoxication two undesirable reactions are encountered, the panic state and the paranoid reaction. The loss of our customary controls, or the idea of having to live forever in a disorganized state, can lead to considerable anxiety and dread. The acute paranoid state develops because LSD produces a hypersuggestible condition in which subjects seriously misinterpret their situation. They may become excessively suspicious or grandiose, the latter being more common. This can culminate in megalomaniacal notions of omniscience and indestructibility for example, subjects' firm convictions that they could fly or walk on water.

"Flashbacks" or brief recurrences of the LSD state weeks or months after the last trip are well known but not well understood. These are apt to occur under conditions of physical or psychic stress, and may be interpreted as a pleasant, free trip. More often flashbacks are scary because no cause for the changes exist, functioning is impaired, and the nagging possibility that one is going mad is disturbing. Flashbacks are not due to a retention of LSD in the body; the chemical is eliminated in 24 hours. They are a learned behavior. People who have had many LSD experiences tend to have them. Under stress, the mind may revert to an LSD-like state that it has previously experienced.

In the period following an LSD exposure, a variety of unsettling emotional problems may arise, but they are all infrequent. Perhaps the most common is a prolonged anxiety state. The user is upset, depressed, and tense. Some aspect of the LSD state may persist, perhaps the time distortion or the changed appearance of things. Some people are afraid to close their eyes because it makes the disturbance worse. Some can carry on, while others are forced to drop out of school or work because they cannot manage.

Chronic psychotic reactions are known during the post-LSD period. Usually they clear within 48 hours, but some are very resistant. The impression is that the individual was prepsychotic and was precipitated into a schizophrenic breakdown by LSD. However, an occasional stable person might decompensate following an LSD reaction. Almost every kind of psychotic break has been seen: hebephrenia, catatonia, and paranoid reactions. In addition, psychotic depressions and mania have also occurred. Chronic paranoia is worth mentioning in further detail. A fixed, erroneous, focal belief is retained after the LSD day that one has been called on to save the world. Other areas of thinking activity are intact, except for the fixed idea that a messianic mission has been acquired.

LSD complications are far less frequent now than they were a few years ago. This is not necessarily due to a decrease in LSD consumption. A folk knowledge about handling adverse conditions has been gained. Furthermore, the abovementioned decrease in the amount of LSD in the "street" tablet provides less intense states and therefore less complications.

Managing the Side Effects

The "bum" trip can almost always be dealt with by reassurance and support in a quiet environment. The suggestibility of the individual should be utilized to calm and relax him. If his attention can be obtained and held, he can be "talked down." Tactile reassurance is very helpful; his hand should be held or stroked. He should keep his eyes open and his attention fixed on a simple object, a light or a flower.

Drugs are rarely needed, but they are effective in quieting the agitated. Intravenous or intramuscular Valium or a barbiturate are effective. Thorazine can also be used if it is certain that only LSD has been swallowed. These drugs can also be given by mouth, but the onset of action is delayed, and the dosage must be sufficient. All sorts of "cures" for the bummer have been advocated. Many of them are based on the placebo effect on a hypersuggestible person. Acute anxiety and panic states are similarly treated except that tranquilizing drugs may have to be continued for days or weeks. Flashbacks also respond to strong reassurance and support. Tranquilizing drugs are occasionally needed. Psychotic reactions are best medicated with Thorazine or Stelazine, and these may be required for months. A few patients are refractory, but do improve following a few electroconvulsive treatments.

It is fascinating how, in a few years, the drug scene changes in major ways. Not very long ago we were concerned about the person who made LSD a career. Now the pure acidhead hardly exists. What has happened? Some who pursued the LSD way of life eventually abandoned it and went on to middle-class work and play, or turned on with alternative activities like meditation. encounter groups, or communal living. Other LSD habitues went over to the amphetamines, cocaine and heroin. and are called polydrug users at present. For some, their LSD period was an important and worthwhile learning event, for others a brief stop on the road to "H."

Therapeutic Uses

One of the unfortunate aspects of the LSD situation is the sharp decrease in scientific human research with the drug. Research is not actually discouraged, but the legal requirements have become so un-wieldly as to be difficult for investigators. Three federal agencies have regulations pertaining to research with hallucinogens. In addition, state, county, university, and departmental approvals are required. As a result, some capable investigators have withdrawn from active research. In addition, public attitudes toward LSD are so polarized that subjects without bias are difficult to find.

The possibility that LSD or something like it may be an aid in the psychotherapeutic process has been examined both here and abroad. The European therapists tend to use small doses (50 to 150 mcg) to explore areas which their patients ordinarily have difficulty dealing with. The hope is that LSD will reduce defensiveness, increase the recall of strongly repressed memories, and enhance the emotional response to the retrieved conflicts. Insights are gained, and the sug-gestible state of the patient makes them doubly impressive. North American therapists who have used LSD generally seek for a transcen-dental state with large doses (200 to 600 mcg). With the loss of ego integrity, and of critical ego function, a sort of psychological death experience occurs from which the patient finds himself reborn with an opportunity to begin a new existence. The out-of-the-body experience also gives the patient a sense of meaning to existence. Alcoholics, drug addicts, and neurotic individuals have been the usual candidates for treatment. The early results were promising, but double-blind, con-trolled studies have been unable to demonstrate a difference between the LSD group and the placebo group when the follow-up period extended beyond a year.

Research has been under way at the Maryland Psychiatric Research Institute and by the author to determine whether a chemical trans-cendental experience has a role to play in helping terminally ill patients who are anguished about their death. These have generally been patients with cancers that have extended beyond hopes of cure. They are often in pain and very depressed. The goal of the LSD treatment is to give the patients a feeling that death is not meaningless, and that their demise is part of a meaningful pattern. About half of such patients benefit. Of those that do, the benefit is reflected in less need for pain medication, a sense of calm about their death, and the ability to make a final peace with their families.

OTHER PSYCHEDELICS

Dimethyltryptamine (DMT)

DMT has been found in cohaba snuff, which is blown into the nose through a bird's hollow wing bone by the Mira Indians. This easily manufactured product has been smoked, snuffed, or injected by some people, but its popularity has waned. The experience is rapid of onset, very intense, and of brief duration. It is too frightening and unpleasant for many who try it. Diethyltryptamine (DET), dipropyltryptamine (DPT), and other related compounds have been made and tested. They all have slightly different hallucinogenic effects, but none seem to be coming into medical or nonmedical use.

Psilocybin

Psilocybin occurs naturally in *Psilocyba mexicana* and related mushrooms. They are highly regarded and have been called the "food of the Gods" by Central American Indians. When LSD was accused of causing chromosomal breaks, users went over to psilocybin and mescaline. When analyzed, however, these turned out to be either LSD or PCP (phencyclidine). Pure psilocybin is very rare on the street. It is used instead of LSD as a therapeutic agent in a small number of clinics particularly in Europe. Psychedelic gourmets believe that they can distinguish between LSD, psilocybin, and mescaline. This has not yet been borne out under controlled conditions.

Peyote and Mescaline

The dried buttons of the peyote cactus are the only hallucinogen legally consumed in this country; it is used by the American Indians of the Native American Church, and permitted because it is a sacrament used within formal, established religious ceremonies. The buttons are bitter and nauseating; mescaline is much more palatable. A great future was predicted for mescaline at the turn of the century by Havelock Ellis and Weir Mitchell, but it never achieved widespread use. Today, essentially none of the material sold as mescaline is that substance.

STP

Named after the motor oil additive, but subsequently transformed into an abbreviation for Serenity, Tranquility, Peace, STP joined the psychedelic list in 1967. During "love-ins," STP was distributed free as a pro-motional pump-priming device. The dose was not precisely calculated, and more adverse effects resulted than from other hallucinogens. In appropriate amounts STP is not more harmful than any other psyche-delic. Like the other street drugs, it is frequently adulterated, and this has led to the false notion that Thorazine makes the side effects worse.

MDA

MDA is a current favorite street psychedelic. Like STP, it is chemically related to amphetamine and mescaline. It is claimed that less audio-visual distortions occur, and more personal examination transpires; therefore it might be of some value in psychotherapy. Careful studies with MDA remain to be carried out.

PCP (Phencyclidine)

This animal tranquilizer apparently reaches the street from illicit laboratories and clinics. Hog and Angel Dust are street names for PCP. It can be either smoked or swallowed. Originally employed as an anesthetic for human surgery, the delirium that occasionally occurred postoperatively made it an undesirable agent. Although PCP has never attracted a large following on its own, it appears in items sold as LSD, mescaline, psilocybin, THC, and even cocaine. It can be thought of as the universal psychedelic adulterant, perhaps because it is readily available in good supply. Its manufacture has caused problems, and an occasional batch that reaches the black market evokes very undesirable side effects. Feelings of emptiness and nothingness are regularly described with PCP. Thorazine should not be used as an antidote for this drug.

THE CHEMICAL TRANSCENDENTAL STATE

There is a unique state of human awareness, variously called a transcendental, mystical, religious, or peak experience, which can be mimicked by a large dose of a psychedelic drug. It consists of intense feelings of awe, wonder, or ecstasy, loss of self, or feelings of union with the universe and visual brilliance (the Great White Light of God). Thought becomes contentless, the impression that something of great profundity and significance is occurring is strong, and time ceases to exist. The spontaneous experience ordinarily develops after periods of severe deprivation or stress, or long periods of strenuous religious devotions. The state induced by a chemical like LSD may have some or all the qualities described above.

It was these dramatic events that attracted and made disciples of so many young people a decade ago, for they found in LSD an experience of meaning seriously lacking in their middle-class lives. In order to understand the fascination of the psychedelics, it is necessary to recognize not only the visual wonders of the trip, but also the chemical transcendental state so impressive to those who experienced it.

PSYCHEDELIC DILEMMAS

There are questions posed by the psychedelic experience to which answers are not clearly available, only informed guesses. Nevertheless, the issues are important enough to raise, and to make an attempt at resolution.

1 *Are the insights gained under LSD true? Is the vision of existence one sees in the LSD state the real reality?* The insights acquired about oneself can be either valid or invalid. Some are obviously erroneous, while others may contain valuable elements that could be helpful if they were used to develop new behaviors. An insight is valueless unless the information is converted into improved living. As to the exact nature of reality, who can tell? Care must be taken to avoid rearranging one's philosophy on the basis of some delusional idea that comes into mind under LSD. The mystics and the philosophers seem to tell us that chemical inspirations and knowledge must be most carefully examined before they are adopted. Furthermore, they say, the effects of the knowledge are much more important than the knowledge itself. "What is done with it?" "How is the life altered?" are their questions.

2 *Doesn't LSD show us how stupid our life games are?* Our games are silly, indeed, but no more so than the games that come from the drug experience. It seems important to be aware of our game-playing existence and to rid ourselves of the more inane roles. A totally nongame life is probably unachievable.

3 *Is the chemical transcendental state the same as the transcendence that comes about through training?* They are similar, but also very different. The natural transcendental state usually comes to those who have prepared themselves for it, perhaps by vigils, medi-

itation, exercises, or strenuous life experience. They are better equipped to handle it, will not be overwhelmed by it, and will learn from it. Those who come upon an enormous transforming experience unprepared may emerge quite unchanged or, indeed, even harmed. Nor is transcendence an end in itself; it is, if anything, a beginning toward a more aware existence.

4 *How should the chemical mystical state be viewed?* It should be seen as a remarkable example of the potential of the mind, and of the varieties of altered states of unconsciousness. Many users of psychedelics have gone beyond the use of drugs to explore themselves and their universe with more valid techniques. Used in this fashion, their psychedelic experience was valuable.

The Psychedelics…
Marihuana

It is only during the past half dozen years that the scientific study of cannabis has fully developed. Much of our previous information has been found to be faulty, and a complete revision of this chapter as it appeared in the first edition has become necessary.

The Plant

Cannabis indica will grow wild or cultivated in any temperate or tropical moist climate. Two major types are found: the fiber and the drug types. The fiber variety is exemplified by the wild North American material. It is low in Δ-9-tetrahydrocannabinol (THC) and high in cannabidiol (CBD). This variety of cannabis was cultivated in the past as a source of rope and cloth. THC is the active ingredient in marihuana, and CBD is without mental activity. The drug type has a high THC and a low CBD content. Good-quality Mexican, Vietnamese, or Nepalese marihuana represents the drug type.

When fiber- and drug-type seeds are grown under identical conditions they will contain the same THC-CBD ratios as the parent plants. Ideal conditions of moisture, fertilization, and sunlight will increase THC content, but hemp-type plants do not achieve the levels of drug-type plants.

It is the flowering tops, the bracts (small green leaves around the flower) and the upper leaves that have the highest THC content. The seeds, stems, and roots contain negligible amounts. Contrary to the folklore, the male plant has as high a THC content as the female plant. It is removed from cultivated fields to prevent fertilization, at which time a sharp loss of THC to inactive cannabinol occurs. Some average THC values for various cannabis materials are: fiber-type cannabis 0.05 percent THC, drug-type cannabis 1 percent THC, hashish 10 percent THC, red oil (marihuana distillate) 20 percent THC.

The THC content of dried and stored plant material slowly decreases. Its loss of potency accelerates when stored at room temperature and exposed to light.

Chemistry and Pharmacology

Pure THC is a sticky substance, highly insoluble in water, but soluble in alcohol, other volatile solvents, and fats. Its half-life in the human being is over two days, because of retention in lipid tissues. It is metabolized in the liver by the addition of hydroxyl groups and eventually excreted in the urine and feces. Studies with radioactive THC show that the brain receives no more than would be anticipated on the basis of its weight. Within the brain some localization in midbrain structures and the frontal and occipital lobes occurs.

The effective dose of THC is about one mg. This can be obtained by smoking a "joint" weighing 500 mg of marihuana containing 1 percent THC. Although 5 mg of THC is contained in the cigarette, only about a fifth of it actually gets into the blood stream. Most is lost in the sidestream smoke in the "roach," by combustion, and by not reaching the lung sacs. Taking marihuana by mouth is even more inefficient. Because of poor solubility, about three times as much must be ingested as smoked to provide an equivalent effect.

THC is a very potent hallucinogenic substance. The infrequent incidence of serious adverse effects from marihuana is due to its low THC content. When 30 mg of THC is given intravenously (equivalent to smoking 30 drug-type marihuana cigarettes) even experienced smokers have developed paranoid psychotic reactions.

The most reliable physiologic changes that accompany the use of ordinary amounts of marihuana are an increased heart rate and a dilation of the blood vessels of the whites of the eyes. The latter is not due to the irritant effects of the smoke since it also develops when cannabis is swallowed. Increases in pulse rate of about 20 beats per minute are regularly measured and the increase parallels the mental effects quite well.

The long-held belief that marihuana dilates the pupils is incorrect. Another incorrect assumption is that the craving for sweets reported by marihuana users is due to low blood sugar. This is incorrect, even though the cause of the hunger feelings noted in about half the users is not precisely known.

Tolerance and withdrawal symptoms do not develop from marihuana as it is used in this country. This is because very few people use high-quality cannabis in large amounts. Tolerance to large amounts of THC is definitely established, and some nonspecific withdrawal symptoms in heavy hashish smokers have been described. Folk experience, along with some research evidence indicates that marihuana and alcohol potentiate each other. The combination of "pot" and sweet wines is particularly favored.

The often mentioned reverse tolerance probably results from improved smoking techniques and a learned ability to identify the early manifestations of the state. It is conceivable that the long retention time in the body also contributes to the need for less pot to provide an equivalent effect. It is well known that the novice may notice no effects from his first exposure to marihuana. The reasons mentioned for reverse tolerance also explain the lack of effect in first-time users. In addition, it may be necessary to build up levels of certain body enzymes in beginners to activate the marihuana constituents. Experienced users do metabolize THC differently from novices. They also learn how to handle the state. Since the smoked THC quickly passes from the lungs into the brain, the smoker can adjust the amount of drug used to correspond to the level of intoxication desired.

A fair part of the marihuana effect is exerted by nondrug factors. "Potheads" have difficulty in evaluating the difference between real marihuana and a placebo if they are unaware that a placebo might be provided. The set the setting the mood of the group all influence the nature and intensity of the state. Suggestibility is strong, not only in the user but also in the nonindulging group members who speak of a "contact high."

A slowing of the alpha rhythm on brain wave tracing is consistent with the drowsiness often experienced. Complex reaction time is slowed, hand steadiness decreased, and time tends to be overestimated. Very recent memory is impaired, and this is reflected in the speech of some users who forget what they just said. Driving skills are impaired, with braking time and recovery from glare most affected.

The "Stoned" State

Ordinary amounts of smoked marihuana are marked by feelings of relaxation, euphoria, and a partial relaxation of controls over emotions and thought. A sort of reverie state may intervene. with colorful fantasy imagery. Time may be slowed and space altered. The critical function of the ego is diminished, making perceptions, thoughts. and feelings seem more intense and real.

In larger amounts the state approaches the intensity produced by psychedelics like LSD. Complete loss of self, paranoid delusions. hallucinatory experiences, and anxiety or panic may be observed. When combinations of drugs are used, the end result becomes difficult to predict.

The state starts a few minutes after properly smoking active marihuana and lasts an hour or two. When cannabis is eaten the onset is delayed, but it may last longer. It is believed that ingestion of the material leads to negative reactions more often than smoking it.

Street supplies have been found to range from completely inactive material to fairly good Mexican marijuana. Adulterations with oregano or dried grass have been detected. Reports of more ominous adulterants like heroin or various poisons have not been confirmed. Marihuana for research purposes is grown at a well-protected site at the University of Mississippi for the National Institute of Drug Abuse. Hashish is entering the country in increasing quantities and an extract of marihuana (hash oil, 20 to 70 percent THC, superpot) is also available.

To this time, the material sold as THC has never been found to be that substance—it turns out to be PCP or LSD. This is not surprising in view of the difficulty of manufacture. Pure THC is made for research purposes and distributed by the National Institute of Drug Abuse to qualified investigators.

Adverse Effects

Adverse effects are infrequent. Headache and sluggishness are mentioned as hangover symptoms. Anxiety and panic reactions and toxic deliria do occur, but usually in inexperienced users. "Flashbacks" such as those reported with LSD have, on rare occasions, been mentioned. What is more common is for persons who have recurrences of their LSD trips to be precipitated into such flashbacks by marihuana. Paranoid episodes may also arise, and some may last for extended periods of time. Whether these prolonged psychotic reactions happen to predisposed individuals is uncertain. Certainly borderline people may decompensate if the cannabis experience happens to be a very intense one.

A number of untoward effects remain matters for discussion and debate. They will be mentioned, and the most recent thinking on their significance will be stated.

The Amotivational Syndrome For centuries countries where cannabis was traditionally used tended to be economically retarded, agrarian rather than industrialized, and in general less involved in scientific and technological revolutions. Some writers blamed the poverty on mass loss of drive due to the widespread use of the drug. More recently, following the observations that young, heavy users of cannabis seemed to lose previous interests, had diminished drives to achieve, and often dropped out, this assertion has been reformulated as the amotivational syndrome. In the case of the backward countries, other factors appear to contribute as much as cannabis intoxication. Poor nutrition, contagious diseases, and overpopulation are among these factors. Studies of dropouts from Western society have generally found that many were marginally adjusted to school or work even before they started using the drug. It is true that one can drop out easier while taking marihuana. It is also true that heavy marihuana users cluster together and reinforce each other's antiachiever beliefs.

The drug does induce relaxation and passivity, but in moderate amounts this state need not interfere with other life interests. When very large amounts are taken, and the pothead is stoned during waking hours, it is easy to understand how future plans, goals, and aspirations will wither away. It is the young pothead whose life revolves around marihuana who is at risk psychologically. Adolescence is a period of learning how to deal with life stress and problems. If these are "solved" by becoming stoned, nothing is learned, and a perpetual immaturity remains. Persons who drop out of the daily "hassle" may do so not so much from choice, but because they feel unable to cope. They have never learned how.

A study done in Jamaica[1] recently throws some light on the point that it is not so much the drug as the reasons why it is taken that determine the resulting behavior. On that island, a majority of the poor, rural males smoke the potent "ganja" that grows there. In addition to its social uses, ganja is employed as an energizer. Laborers and farmers will smoke before starting to work in order to feel more energetic and stave off fatigue.

Chromosomal Damage The issue of chromosomal breakage has been raised, primarily as a result of a study at the University of Utah. The study reported an increased rate of chromosomal abnormalities, apparently unrelated to the extent of the use of the drug. No claim was made about fetal damage or the development of cancer. In contrast, most of the other investigators have noted no differences between control and marihuana-using groups. In fact, the Third Annual Report on Marihuana and Health from H.E.W. in 1973 said: "One of the most important findings this year has been to confirm in animal studies that synthetic or natural marihuana appears to have no serious deleterious effects on pregnancy, the fetus or the newborn. While such evidence cannot categorically rule out such effects in humans, it is nevertheless reassuring."

Cancer of the Lung Since marihuana and tobacco both contain coal tars, it is proper to inquire into the cancer-producing potential of the former drug. Marihuana is smoked in a manner that brings the material into deeper areas of the lung for longer periods. However less marihuana is smoked than tobacco. Chronic bronchitis in connection with heavy hashish smoking has been documented. Examination of the bronchial cells show definite changes, but no cancer cells have been found. Long-term studies in animals exposed to marihuana smoke are under way.

Decreased Testosterone Levels Recent studies indicate that regular male users of marihuana (three or more times weekly) have lowered

[1]M. H. Beaubrum and F. Knight, "Psychiatric Assessment of 30 Chronic Users and 30 Matched Controls," *American Journal of Psychiatry*, **130**: 309–311, March 1973.

blood levels of testosterone. In some cases, sperm counts were decreased and a small number of the subjects reported impotence. Further work is needed, but at present the condition is considered a reversible impairment of the hormones in the brain that stimulate gonadal testosterone production.

Impaired Immune Response A report from Nahas[2] indicated that marihuana users have a markedly impaired immune response. The degree of loss of immunity reaction was marked, and of serious nature. If the findings are confirmed, they would imply lowered resistance to infections and cancers. In another study,[3] marihuana smokers had a normal immune response as compared to nonsmokers of the same age group.

The Stepping-Stone Theory A major objection to marihuana use was that it might lead to more dangerous drugs. More than 70 percent of heroin addicts, for example, smoked cannabis prior to going over to heroin. Surveys have indicated that marihuana use is associated with the later use of hallucinogens. However, there is nothing in the pharmacologic activity of cannabis that causes a progression to other drugs. Rather, it is the fact that taking any illegal drug will permit the user to try others. Tobacco and alcohol use ordinarily precede marihuana experimentation.

Marihuana, Crime, and Violence An association between marihuana and criminality has been claimed, but no solid evidence supports this relationship. A similar assertion concerning marihuana-induced violent behavior is likewise unsupported. In a study done for the Marihuana Commission,[4] violence occurred under the influence of marihuana at a lower rate than for other abused drugs.

Marihuana and Brain Damage Reports of marihuana smokers who manifest confusion, recent memory impairment, apathy, and reduced interaction with others, continue to appear. It is heavy smokers of

[2] G. G. Nahas et al., "Inhibition of Cellular Mediated Immunity in Marihuana Smokers," *Science*, 183: 419, 1974.

[3] M. Silverstein and P. Lessin, "Normal Skin Responses in Chronic Marihuana Users, *Science*, 188: 71–72. 1975.

[4] J. Tinklenberg, "Drug and Crime," in *Drug Use in America: Problem in Perspective*, Second Report of the National Commission on Marihuana and Drug Abuse, Appendix 1: 242–299, Washington, D.C., 1973.

potent forms that seem particularly susceptible. In addition, these people are generally users of many other drugs, and are using excessively because of underlying personality problems. This was the nature of the population in one study[5] that found brain atrophy in their cannabis users.

Those who are concerned with the mental effects of marihuana claim that the intellectual impairment is a subtle one that cannot be noticed by the users themselves. Even those close to them can hardly notice a chance except over a period of months. They cite instances of users who stop and then declare after a drug-free period that their thinking is clearer. It is difficult to prove such minor alterations in thinking ability, because the ordinary demands of existence rarely require our total mental ability.

Therapeutic Potential

Observations made during the past few years indicate a basis for a therapeutic role for cannabis, THC, or a nonintoxicating, related cannabinoid. Such drugs have been found to lower intraocular pressure and may be suitable in the treatment of certain glaucoma patients. A bronchodilating action is present, and it is being tested in bronchial asthma patients. Their relaxing, sedative, appetite-enhancing, and anti-nausea properties are being studied. There is reason to believe that a cannabinoid could be used in the treatment of certain epileptic conditions, and to alter the perception of pain. All of these possibilities remain experimental, but active research is under way.

Legal Trends

The tendency in this country is to reduce penalties for possession and use of small amounts of cannabis while retaining felony statutes against larger-scale dealers. At present, federal and many state laws provide misdemeanor penalties for simple possession. Oregon and a few local communities have reduced the penalty to the consumer to a violation. The recommendation of the President's Commission on Marihuana to decriminalize private use and possession of small quantities of the drug is consistent with what we now know of its harmful effects. Decriminal-

---

[5] A. M. G. Campbell et al., "Cerebral Atrophy in Young Cannabis Smokers," *Lancet*, 2: 1219–1226, 1971.

ization retains the illegal status of the drug for traffickers, but avoids the drastic punishments which have been meted out to the user.

Until a satisfactory answer is obtained regarding its cancer-producing potential, its genetic effects, and similar public health issues, it would be prudent to withhold the legalization of cannabis. The full acceptance of a social drug by a culture seems to be an irreversible process. Once it is accepted little can be done to eliminate the drug if it turns out to be a substantial health hazard.

Consequences of Legalization

A number of developments can be predicted if cannabis is legalized in a manner similar to our treatment of alcohol.

1 The number of users will increase. Surveys indicate that about 10 percent of students and larger numbers of older adults do not smoke because it is illegal. On the other hand, those who smoke predominantly as a protest against the Establishment may stop.

2 As total numbers increase, the number of heavy users will increase.

3 The strength of the cannabis used will increase. This trend is already noticeable, with more hashish being consumed now than in the past. No doubt, one day, pure THC will become available outside the research laboratory. Legalization would probably not include the stronger cannabis preparations.

4 It will still be illegal to sell to minors, but they will become involved in greater numbers than at present.

5 The consumption of alcoholic beverages will not decrease. At one time the substitution of marihuana for alcohol was put forth as an argument for legalization. More recently it has become clear that marihuana users also consume their share of alcoholic beverages.

6 The smoking of tobacco products will be relatively unaffected. There have been no signs of a shift away from tobacco by cannabis users.

7 Increased federal and state revenues will accrue. About a billion dollars a year in taxes and fees would result from regulating marihuana. Less than 10,000 acres would grow the amount needed to supply domestic requirements.

Chapter 5

Amphetamines, Cocaine, and Other Stimulants

The stimulants (uppers, pep pills) were widely abused during the early 1970s. Now, because of increasing prescription controls, the trend toward depressant drugs, and the sheer exhaustion that accompanies using stimulants in large amounts over long periods, stimulants have leveled off or even declined. Their medical indications include the treatment of mild depressions and fatigue states, narcolepsy, and hyperkinetic behavioral disorders of children. They can also be used in short courses for weight reduction, and for preventing drowsiness under emergency conditions where sleep is undesirable. Amphetamines have been rather widely used to deal with short-term, strenuous mental or physical efforts like examinations and sport races. The research evidence reveals that performance is not improved unless fatigue is present. In sustained physical endurance events such as competitive athletic contests, performance may be enhanced, but judgment is impaired. In long-distance bicycle races and long-distance swimming events, athletes have been known to overtax their hearts when the signs of exhaustion and circulatory failure were masked by stimulant drugs.

The Most Common Stimulants

Trade name	Generic name	Street name	Abuse potential
1 *Amphetamines*			
Dexedrine	dextroamphetamines	dexies	high
Benzedrine	amphetamine	bennies	high
Methedrine	methamphetamine	splash, crank, meth, crystal	high
2 *Amphetaminelike antiobesity agents*			
Preludin	phenmetrazine	—	high
Tenuate, Tepanil	diethylproprion	—	low
Ionamine	phentermine	—	low
Pre-Sate	chlorphentermine	—	low
3 *Others*			
Ritalen	methyphenidate	—	high
Meretran	pipradrol	—	low
Cocaine	cocaine hydrochloride	snow, coke	high

Patterns of Abuse

Two patterns of abuse can be distinguished: the consumption of small amounts over long periods, and the swallowing or injecting of very large quantities. In the first instance a person might be placed on anti-obesity pills for weight reduction or on an amphetamine for chronic tiredness. After a few weeks, tolerance develops and a few more pills are needed. The lift in energy level and feeling of exhilaration are relished, and users are unwilling to give up taking the medication. Or they may find that if they do, the fatigue and apathy are worse than ever, and they quickly resume their stimulant. Average amounts probably can be taken over long periods without serious consequences, but if the dose continues to be increased, untoward effects can occur.

The consistent use of very large amounts might be called the "speed-freak" phenomenon. After the acquisition of tolerance one hundred times the average dose can be injected intravenously at one time. The immediate "rush" or "flash" is described as being like a maximal stimulus to the pleasure center of the brain. After the immediate reaction, a feeling of energy and well-being continues, and then gradually diminishes. Additional injections of amphetamines are taken and a "speed run" is under way. After a few days, exhaustion of the individuals or of their supplies requires that they "crash." This abrupt discontinuance produces a characteristic withdrawal syndrome. Having not slept during this period they may proceed to sleep for a day or more. Having not eaten, they will eat ravenously. The cardinal symptom of the stimulant withdrawal syndrome, however, is a profound psychological depression. The low is as low as the high was high. It is at this point that a suicide might occur. The "speed freak" soon learns that the depression can be lifted by a reinjection of amphetamines. This is the start of another speed run, and partly explains why such people are difficult to treat.

Some other features of the high dose amphetamine state require mention. Paranoid thinking is universal. Pathological suspiciousness is the rule in contrast to the grandiosity of the hallucinogenic state. Ideas that one is being followed, watched, or persecuted can result in flight or fighting behavior. Innocent people have been assaulted under these conditions. The best model of paranoid schizophrenia can be created by the use of increasing amounts of amphetamines, even in normal subjects.

A peculiar repetitive behavior is often encountered. Simple acts such as washing a floor, stringing and unstringing beads, or pacing to and fro are carried on for hours. Such stereotyped behaviors are also observed in every animal species given amphetamines. Stereotypy may account for some bizarre deaths in which the person is stabbed hundreds of times. Other elements of the high-dose state can make users violent. They are irritable, impulsive, and overactive. In drug-using circles they are known to be unpredictable and completely untrustworthy.

Amphetamines will dilate the pupils and raise blood pressure, body temperature, and respiratory rate. Tendon reflexes are quickened and a tremulousness occurs. Considerable weight loss and malnutrition accompany a few speed runs. By that time the freak looks like a concentration camp inmate. A curious condition, called "overamping" on the street follows extremely large amounts of speed. It consists of the inability to move or talk even though consciousness is retained. Perhaps it is related to a catatonic immobility. Death, when it occurs, is from heat stroke or from the rupture of a blood vessel in the brain due to the elevated blood pressure. It is the most frequent cause of cerebral hemorrhage in young people these days. Amphetamines are sometimes taken, less for the high than for the enhancement of sexual activity. Orgasm and ejaculation are delayed or may never come about. Libido is increased, and hypersexuality is frequent.

Epidemics of amphetamine abuse took place in other countries prior to our involvement with them. In Japan, after World War II, the collapse of the traditional social and economic order set the stage for an amphetamine epidemic. To earn a living, long, hard hours had to be worked. At the same time large stockpiles of military supplies were released. In some urban areas 5 percent of workers between 15 and 25 years of age became dependent on amphetamines. In the year 1954 alone, 55,000 arrests were made in Japan for amphetamine possession or sale, and many paranoid psychoses were reported in the Japanese scientific literature. Strict controls over the drug and mandatory treatment procedures led to a decline in prevalence. More recently, Japanese juveniles have rediscovered stimulant overuse.

The Swedish problem began 10 years ago and continues today. The weight control medication, Preludin, was alleged to be nonhabit-forming, and it could be purchased without a prescription. A small number of *avant garde* Stockholm artists enjoyed its effects and discovered the enhanced attraction of intravenous instillation. The practice spread until 10,000 people (out of a population of 8 million) were considered dependent upon Preludin and amphetamines. An attempt to control the spread by providing the drugs legally failed. Increasingly severe controls over medical and nonmedical supplies have curtailed, but not eliminated the problem.

In the United States the amphetamines have been placed in Schedule II.[1] Special prescription forms are needed, and these are not refillable. Many doctors have voluntarily given up the legitimate prescribing of these drugs. However, amphetamines are readily made from precursors that are not difficult to obtain.

---

[1] Schedule I: Drugs with high potential for abuse and no medical usefulness, e.g., heroin.

Schedule II: Drugs with high potential for abuse but with medical usefulness, e.g., morphine.

Schedule III: Drugs with moderate potential for abuse and with medical usefulness, e.g., barbiturates.

Schedule IV: Drugs with low potential for abuse and with medical usefulness, e.g., Valium.

Schedule V: Exempt narcotics, e.g., codeine cough mixtures.

Ritalen and Preludin

Ritalen is a stimulant used in medicine for mild depressions, narcolepsy, minimal brain dysfunction, and sedative-induced lethargy. Sporadic epidemics of Ritalen abuse appear, depending upon illicit supplies. The clinical picture is similar, but perhaps smoother, than amphetamine misuse. One special problem is that Ritalen tablets have talcum as a binder. Talc is insoluble and a tissue irritant. Used intravenously, it causes inflammation and scarring of the lungs.

Preludin is almost exclusively employed for weight control. Its abuse is infrequent in this country. Some stimulant-dependent people prefer it to amphetamines, others declare that they are equivalent in action.

Cocaine

If other stimulant abuse has been decreasing, that of cocaine has not. It is increasingly being used alone and in combination with depressant drugs. Confiscation of larger amounts at the national border is increasingly reported in the media these days. The leaves of the coca bush (*Eryththroylon coca*) have been chewed in the northern Andes for thousands of years. In the beginning this was a luxury reserved for the ruling Incas. Later, the Indians who worked the tin and silver mines were provided with it as part of their pay because it suppressed hunger and reduced fatigue. Today, it is claimed that 90 percent of the men and 20 percent of the women who live in the thin air of the two-mile-high mountains chew coca. The leaves contain about 1 percent cocaine, and its first extraction occurred over a hundred years ago. Sigmund Freud was one of its earliest investigators, and he praised its ability to allay depression and pain. His enthusiasm subsided after his best friend became a compulsive cocainist. Cocaine was contained in a number of patent medicines and soft drinks until the Pure Food and Drug Law was enacted. Its usefulness as a local anesthetic has been superceded since safer synthetic compounds have been introduced.

What has been said about paranoid thought disorders and other effects resulting from amphetamines applies also to cocaine. One additional peculiarity is the "cocaine bugs" or "crankbugs" which the confirmed user will sometimes hallucinate crawling under the skin. This leads to scratching and ulcerations. The membranes of the nose are irritated by constant cocaine sniffing, and can eventually ulcerate.

Tolerance to cocaine does not develop, perhaps because it is metabolized so rapidly in the body. Therefore, a withdrawal syndrome after sudden stoppage of the drug is unknown. One should not speak of addiction to cocaine, since the features of addiction as defined are not present. The problem with stopping use of cocaine after frequent exposures comes from the strong psychological desire to repeat the experience. People who sample cocaine on one or a few occasions have little difficulty in abstaining when supplies are not at hand. The use of cocaine, then, is an instance of a nonaddicting drug being abused by certain people on the basis of their craving for it. It is, therefore, not rational to equate the absence of addiction with harmlessness.

Another difference between amphetamines and cocaine is the brief duration of action of the latter. Cocaine snorted or injected intravenously will last only a few minutes because it is rapidly broken down in the body. Amphetamines taken in the same way have an effect for many hours. Thus the cocaine rush can be obtained dozens or hundreds of times a day by repeated usage. The amphetamine rush can be achieved only a half-dozen times a day with the subsequent "glow" lasting for hours. It is the indescribable rush that is sought after, therefore cocaine is preferred by stimulant users to the amphetamines. The short action of cocaine also avoids much but not all of the violent behavior seen with the amphetamines.

Cocaine, a few years ago the drug of musicians and artists, has now spread beyond these groups to many other consumers. It is sampled by students who want to try everything, by certain of their faculty as the current "in" drug, and by what used to be called the *avant garde*. At this time cocaine use remains an urban phenomenon, and cities like New York, Miami (the port of entry for much of the material), Chicago, San Francisco, and Los Angeles are particularly involved.

Due to its high price ($2,000 an ounce) cocaine has been adulterated with strychnine, amphetamines, and other substances in recent years. Samples may contain as little as 5 percent cocaine on the street. Various patterns of usage can be discerned. The pure "cokehead" must have a lucrative source of income in order to afford the rich man's speed. Polydrug users will try cocaine when they can get it, but will employ other agents for everyday use. The "speedball artist" has already been mentioned. British heroin users were sometimes given cocaine, but it is no longer prescribed. It has been found that some patients in methadone maintenance programs have taken to cocaine for their highs since the action of heroin is blocked by methadone.

The stimulant-dependent person is a difficult problem in treatment. He often leaves the treatment situation, or relapses back to stimulant use. As satisfactory a program as any for the speed freak has been compulsory commitment to a facility where ex-users will accept him into a therapeutic community setting. Detoxification is easy, but the prevention of relapse is difficult and prolonged. The management of cocaine or amphetamine overdose includes the support of vital functions and the administration of a drug like Thorazine, which is a physiological antagonist. The withdrawal from stimulants, although strenuous, is not life-endangering. Gradual reduction of dosage is not necessary. The experienced user may take a sedative or heroin to help avoid the discomfort. For the psychological depression an antidepressant may be indicated.

Chapter 6

The Narcotics

HISTORY

The story of opium is fascinating, but only those facets will be mentioned that contribute to an understanding of our current predicament. Opium was in use for thousands of years before its addictive ability was appreciated. The Asian peasant smoking his opium pipe was tied to his habit, but supplies were sufficient, and his way of life did not require complicated thinking or vigilance. His dreamy, passive state harmed no one, and it served as a refuge from the raw misery of the day. It was otherwise when gum opium and laundanum (tincture of opium) came into the marketplaces of the busy cities of the Western world. There the pace was quicker alertness was essential, and clear-headed functioning was a requirement. Opium-dependent urban users, their families, and their communities were impaired by the incapacitating effects of the narcotic.

Opium "eating" was a middle- and upper-class phenomenon at the end of the eighteenth century in England. In certain ways. opium use during that period and the recent wave of psychedelic use in this country have interesting similarities. In both instances the problem was blamed on the difficult, unsettled, depressing times. Many of the elite were involved. DeQuincey was most closely identified with opium because of his *Confessions of an English Opium Eater.* Poe, Coleridge, Swinburne, and Elizabeth Barrett Browning thought of it as the final answer to man's ills, but later they all changed their minds.

The widespread use of laudanum was also seen in nineteenth century America. Many patent medicines were laced with it, and because of the inadequacies of medical care, most diseases were self-treated with pain-relieving medicaments. Women were especially liable to become dependent upon some pain reliever. Even babies' soothing syrups contained a tot's share. Infants become irritable and cried when deprived of their soothing syrup a symptom of early withdrawal. Another source of the opium habit was the custom the Chinese laborers brought with them. After a day's work on the transcontinental railroad or the placer mines of the Mother Lode country, an evening with a pipe and a few pellets of smoking opium was relaxing. The practice spread from the dens of Chinatown to the sporting bloods, the prostitutes, and even to the youths of respectable middle-class families.

After morphine, the major alkaloid, was extracted from opium in the 1850s. the addiction problem escalated. At about that time the hypodermic syringe was invented. It was now possible to bypass the less efficient routes of ingestion and inject morphine directly under the skin or even into the bloodstream. It was during the Civil War, when thousands were suffering from painful wounds, malaria, and dysentery, that morphine injections were dispensed liberally to those who sought relief. By this time it was known that opium eating or smoking could cause addiction. But somehow it was believed that giving pure morphine under the skin would avoid addiction. In fact, the contrary was true. Injected morphine causes physical addiction sooner and more intensely than opium. The tragic story was not yet ended. In 1898 morphine was treated with strong acetic acid. The early trials with the resulting compound indicated that it was a potent pain reliever, and that it cured both opium and morphine addiction. It was received with enthusiasm and high hopes. It was named heroin.

A hundred years ago the United States had over a million opiate addicts. This was 2 percent of the population. Today only about one person in five hundred (0.2 percent) is addicted to some opiate.

However, although percentages have decreased, the nature of narcotic addiction has worsened. The less addicting oral opium has been replaced by contaminated intravenous heroin. The criminalization of opiate addiction has degraded the addict and imposed a vast criminal infrastructure on society.

Three lessons can be learned from the foregoing brief account. One is that it may take a long time before the adverse effects of a drug become apparent. Each new agent seems much better than the known drugs because we are aware of the hazards of the latter and not yet cognizant with those of the former. The addictive potential of opium was not recognized for millenia. When morphine became available, it was used to cure opium dependence, and heroin in its turn cured addictions to the then established drugs. Another lesson to be learned is that a change in the cultural setting or in the manner which the drug is taken causes entirely new problems. Smoking a pipeful of opium on a remote farm in the Asian hinterland is hardly comparable to "shooting up" heroin in a metropolis. Finally, it must be recognized that when middle- or upper-class intellectuals introduce a drug fad, it is likely to be as poor a choice as when it seeps out of the ghetto. The intelligentsia are not very intelligent in these matters.

OPIATES

Opium is obtained from the gum that oozes out of the cut, unripe pod of the Oriental poppy (*Papaver somniferum*). The common alkaloids derived from opium are morphine and codeine with heroin being made from morphine. A number of synthetic drugs act like morphine. They include methadone, Demerol, and Dilaudid. All opiates are dependence-producing, but some are high in this respect (heroin), while others are low (codeine). The main item in illicit commerce is heroin in cellophane "decks," "bags," or capsules. Its quality is highly variable, and 5 percent heroin is considered a good buy. At times it is so weak that true addiction cannot occur: instead the person becomes conditioned to the way of life and the ritual of the "fix." Heroin is cut by a succession of dealers who use milk sugar, baking soda, and quinine. Analysis of various samples obtained from "pushers" in one city revealed a span from 0 to 77 percent heroin, with most samples being in the lowest range. It is clear that if an addict happens to obtain insufficiently cut heroin he may overdose with it since his tolerance is not great enough to manage such an amount. Heroin has no medical use in this country. The entire supply is brought in from the Middle East, the Far East, or Mexico.

Morphine has been the standard pain reliever for the past century. It is about a third as potent as full-strength heroin. Morphine addiction is much less frequently encountered than it used to be; a patient with a painful illness may become addicted, or a doctor or nurse acquire the habit. When morphine appears on the street, it is from drugstore robberies or faked prescriptions. Heroin is excreted as morphine in the urine. One day equally good analgesia will be obtained by some synthetic compound which does not produce dependence, and the need for morphine in medicine will disappear.

Codeine is used as an analgesic for less painful conditions. Its addiction potential is much less than morphine. It is not highly regarded by heroin addicts, but when they become separated from their connection, they may resort to codeine in the form of cough syrups. There is a tendency to replace the codeine in cough syrups with dextromethorphan, which is almost nonaddictive and a good cough suppressant, but some codeine mixtures are still available.

Demerol is a widely used pain reliever that is only a little less addictive than morphine. Addicts have been created by the careless use of Demerol by physicians. If a painful illness is sure to result in death within a short time there is no reason to withhold analgesics like Demerol or morphine. However, chronic pain that will last for years is a vastly different matter. It must be treated with the greatest skill to provide relief and yet avoid addiction. Dilaudid and Pantopon are other opiates with a definite addiction potential. Before a person becomes addicted to these potent narcotics it is necessary for him to take pain-relieving amounts a number of times a day for at least a week. By that time he will have developed tolerance, and if the drug is stopped, withdrawal symptoms will be experienced.

Methadone is another synthetic narcotic, which will be discussed in detail because of its wide use for detoxification and maintenance of heroin addicts. L-alpha-acetylmethadol (LAAM) is a long-acting form of methadone (2 to 3 days) which is being used to eliminate the need for the daily doses of methadone. When methadone is seen on the black market, it has been diverted from clinics where it is used for maintenance.

THE HEROIN ADDICT

The heroin addict of the 1970s is likely to be a member of a minority, but often enough is a middle-class white. It is probable that the addict is male (the ratio used to be 5:1) but females are becoming addicted in increasing numbers. He is ordinarily in his 20s or 30s, but subteenager and geriatric addicts are well known. His habit may cost from 10-200 dollars a day, and he will inject himself three to six times in 24 hours. It is the need to "hustle" (obtain the funds to "score" or "cop") and to "fix" that requires his entire waking energies. In a minority of instances enough money to provide for the habit can be earned legitimately. Generally, illegal pursuits supplement or replace work as a source of funds. Traditionally, these consist of "pushing," prostitution, shop-lifting, and breaking and entering. Recently, more violent illicit operations have been undertaken by addicts, for example, armed robbery and homicides.

The causes of narcotic addiction are multiple and often complex:

1 An opiate must be available for continuing use.

2 The peers must be using, and often pressures are exerted to make all members of the peer group conform to the practice. This is an important aspect of the introduction to and the perpetuation of addiction. Far more important than the pusher in the spread of addiction is the recently addicted friend. He is the active proselytizor who can start a miniepidemic in his neighborhood. The newly addicted still feels the euphoria and has not yet begun to encounter the miserable aspects of the habit.

3 The family is often in a disorganized state, either nonexistent, broken, or providing a role model of addiction to narcotics, alcohol, or other substances. In some instances, however, the family is intact, loving, and apparently ideal. (It should be remembered that familial influences are no longer as strong as those of peers.)

4 The social situation is one which makes the bedrugged state seem preferable to the sober one. The young person feels hopeless about his situation and helpless about altering it. He has no goals that would provide an alternative to the drug life. Living in a slum may offer little that is rewarding and much that is demoralizing. The youngster in suburbia may be bored, without meaningful or maturing activities, and without the ability to test and know himself. Lack of direction seems to be the disorder common to the affluent and deprived addict alike.

5 Not everyone exposed to peers who want them to try heroin, impossible family situations, and miserable social conditions will become addicted. Personality factors play a role. The so-called addictive personality does not exist, but some people are more vulnerable than others. It is the individual who has a low tolerance for frustration and a high anxiety level, and who is overwhelmed by the ordinary stresses of life who finds great relief from psychic pain in heroin. It is known that many young people will try drugs, including heroin, but those who feel enormously better will stay with them. The inadequate will feel adequate, the schizoid less alone, the shy less shy.

6 Tribal taboos exist that tend to deter certain unacceptable behaviors. The taboo against taking illicit drugs was once strong; now it is weak. The taboo against sticking oneself with a needle and injecting material into one's vein was once very strong; now it is less so. These interdictions once were barriers to addiction; now they hardly exist among some groups.

7 Studies have shown that novices are recruited into trying heroin by friends, sometimes by relatives. The most active recruiter is the addict of short duration who still may get high and who has not yet begun to suffer from cyclic withdrawal or overdose episodes. Another recruiter is the person who is beginning to have trouble supporting his habit. An addicted male will regularly turn his girlfriend on to heroin.

It must be remembered that one injection does not make an addict. Weekend "joy poppers" or "chippers" inject themselves under the skin a day or two a week without developing tolerance. Unfortunately, the nature of the human and of heroin is such that the weekend extends until it finally lasts a week.

The career of the heroin addict should be understood as a full-time occupation that demands considerable skill to survive, time-occupying rituals, defiance of the system, and the benefits of not needing to become deeply involved with anyone. For a few individuals the life is so attractive that they enter into it without using heroin. A condition called "pseudoheroinism" has been described which consists of participating in all the "junkie" activities, but shooting water or extremely diluted "junk." For heroin users with access to the drug, the life seems far better than their previous existence. As time goes on, as their health fails and their friends are gone, as they experience a few "cold turkeys" in jail and nothing is left except the habit, it becomes more and more onerous. Eventually they get too tired, too old to keep up, and they may mature out of the heroin game, either by "kicking" spontaneously or going into a treatment situation. Only small numbers of addicts remain addicted by the time they are 50.

Physical and Psychological Effects

The "total body orgasm" effect so often described following the first few heroin injections is overstated. Some addicts will report never having experienced anything like such a "rush." A feeling of "high" is routinely mentioned, and it seems to represent a warm glow, a sense of relaxation, and a pleasant fantasy experience. As tolerance develops, less and less of the positive effects are perceived. This is particularly true with the weak heroin generally available. After a few years most addicts seem more concerned with avoiding the "sickness" than with the anticipation of a great rush. This is a curious situation: now they are using not to get high, but to stay relatively normal.

Manifestations of heroin use include contraction of the pupils, a reduction in heart rate, breathing, and blood pressure, a loss of all drives, including sex, a decrease in intestinal mobility resulting in constipation, perspiration, and drowsiness ("on the nod"). Work is not well performed if the heroin dose is being increased; however, if the dose is stable the person may perform relatively normally. Nutrition is impaired, not only because the appetite diminishes, but also because the money goes for narcotics. Money spent on food is considered wasted. Women may experience a dimunition or loss of menses. After a short-lived increase, the libido is generally reduced or absent. Addicts with a sufficient amount of heroin in them are content to remain quiet and unobtrusive. If their last fix was eight or more hours ago, they will become restless and energetic in attempting to find heroin.

The sudden discontinuance of a substantial heroin intake leads to profound physiologic changes. Every orifice pours forth its secretion or excretion. Muscles twitch, jerk, pain, or cramp. The muscle spasms may be so pronounced that the extremity will jump involuntarily ("kicking the habit"). Gooseflesh is a reliable objective sign of the withdrawal state. The person may shiver and feel cold or feverish. The pupils are dilated, a nightmarish sleep ("yen sleep") may intervene. Involuntary ejaculations of sperm have been known to occur. Major convulsions are seen. Death is infrequent except in those with serious medical conditions. It is evident that the person undergoing withdrawal will attempt to do anything to obtain relief, and an injection of heroin will provide that relief. What has been described is the classic withdrawal pattern, and it is rarely seen today. People undergoing withdrawal without any medication have some of these symptoms, but they are attenuated. Much of what is experienced these days are symptoms of anxiety or bids for additional amounts of a drug.

The above-described symptoms gradually abate over two or three days, and physical dependence is lost. Psychological craving remains for a long time. Research evidence indicates that even after addicts have recovered and feel well, their physiologic reactions are altered for months, perhaps years. This, plus the conditioning that makes them equate an injection with relief of tension, makes complete recovery difficult but by no means unobtainable.

Complications

If pure and germ-free heroin were available to the consumer, if the technique of injection assured complete sterility, and if tolerance did not develop, then most of the diseases of the junkie could be avoided. In real life none of these criteria are met. Therefore we see disastrous results of persistent heroin usage. The length of life of addicts is far shorter than that of nonusers, and while alive they are beset with a series of illnesses.

One group of complications consists of infections from contaminated drugs or syringes. These result in bacterial or viral infections, which can impinge on the heart valves or anywhere else in the body. The virus of serum hepatitis is transmitted in this manner, and few addicts are spared from at least one bout of hepatitis. The common sharing of "the works" makes for epidemics of hepatitis. This can result in permanent liver damage or in death. In England, where pure heroin and sterile, disposable syringes are provided free by the National Health Service, hepatitis occurs with the same frequency as in the United States. This would be difficult to understand were it not for the observation that the English addicts do not bother to maintain sterile conditions for their injection. This may be a reflection either of the addict's personality, or of what addiction does to the personality.

Another set of problems result from insults to the lung. Solid particles are not infrequently injected, and they lodge in the lung. Sometimes talc or starch is used to cut the heroin, and these substances are insoluble in water. Even straining may not help, since cotton fibers have been found in the lung at autopsy. Pneumonia and tuberculosis are frequent among addicts. Other infections also occur: phlebitis along a vein, skin abcesses, malaria, syphilis, and tetanus following the injection of contaminated material. Addicts are prone to many conditions because of their way of life. Their food intake is haphazard and unbalanced, their teeth lack ordinary attention to say nothing of formal dental care, and skin infections due to dirt and scratching are not uncommon. Because of low general resistance, they heal poorly. The female addict is an excellent candidate for all the venereal diseases and for experiencing physical trauma.

The major cause of death is called overdose (O.D.). In some instances it is just that: more heroin than the person can take without his or her breathing center being knocked out. This can happen when tolerance has been lost and the addict takes what may have been an acceptable dose in the past. It may occur when the addict accidentally obtains a "bag" of very good heroin. It has been known to happen when the pusher deliberately sells a "hot shot," (a known, large dose, or one containing poison). Other reactions are also called overdose. The lungs fill up with fluid, and death occurs within minutes. This may be an allergic reaction to something in the injection. About 1 to 2 percent of addicts are believed to die from acute affects of heroin each year. Narcotic deaths are the major causes of death in people 15 to 35 years of age in New York City. This figure includes methadone and multiple drug fatalities.

Treatment

The rehabilitation of narcotic addicts is not easy for them or for those trying to help. A number of modalities have been developed, and these will be briefly described.

1 Methadone Detoxification Detoxification is the rapid removal of the patient from all narcotics. The technique consists of reducing the usual amount taken by about 10 to 20 percent a day until the person is free of drugs. Methadone is the agent most frequently used, because it can be given by mouth. Other narcotics and tranquilizers have also been used. Little or no withdrawal effects are noted by the patients and hopefully they begin their rehabilitation at this time. Unfortunately, detoxification alone does not produce lasting abstinence. Only 5 percent of those detoxified remain clean. The remainder either relapse or require a more prolonged treatment program.

2 Methadone Maintenance (MM) Some authorities believe that if addicts can be relieved of their craving for heroin for a protracted period of time, they may acquire the psychological resources to remain drug-free. Methadone, which manifests cross-tolerance to heroin, will eliminate heroin hunger and, if given in sufficient amounts, will block the euphoria of intravenous heroin. It has the advantage of being effective by mouth, and of being active over a 24-hour period. Maintaining a patient on methadone at a fixed dose permits him to work, study, drive a car and otherwise function well. MM holds the individual in treatment and provides an opportunity for a reeducational process. With skillful counseling, job-finding, and other restructuring activities, he may eventually be slowly withdrawn from methadone and become drug-free. Some authorities see no objection to continuing methadone for a lifetime. They have placed heroin addicts on the drug for over 10 years without any evidence of toxicity. The philosophy of other doctors is to use methadone to hold patients in treatment. After they show evidence of a new lifestyle and prolonged freedom from other drugs, they are given the opportunity to eliminate the methadone slowly and under clinic control.

It must be clearly understood that, while on MM, the client remains addicted to a narcotic. However, no dirty material is being injected, and one dose of methadone a day takes care of the narcotic requirement. It seems like a desirable substitute for heroin addiction for those who cannot make it in abstinence programs. The results of MM are good in well-run programs, not so good in the others. Of the 60,000 to 80,000 patients in MM, up to 50 percent will do well. Most of the failures turn to alcohol, or take barbiturates to excess. Methadone has appeared on the street, generally from patients who sell off their take-home supplies. In some cities this has been a very considerable problem. The diversion of methadone has led to a renewed interest in a longer-acting methadone which will obviate the need for take-home supplies.

3 Therapeutic Communities (TCs) The ultimate goal for the heroin addict is a drug-free existence that is rewarding and meaningful. Since addicts know the self-deceptions and manipulations that other addicts use, the process of change is best carried out in a company of ex-addicts. The idea of the TC is that throughout the waking day addicts are surrounded by others like them, and each can help the other grow up. Synanon was the first TC for the addicted, and it has been copied and adapted around the world. Living-in is required, and nonuse of drugs and nonviolence are cardinal rules. Mature behavior is rewarded, and childish acts are punished by loss of privileges or by having to perform demeaning tasks. TCs would be the ideal solution for the addict were it not that only the motivated enter them and only the most highly motivated graduate. It has been estimated that no more than 10 to 20 percent of addicts will enter a TC and less than half will complete their reeducation. For those who stay the results are excellent. Many have become leaders in helping other addicts clean up and reconstruct their lives. The need for this mode of treatment is underscored by the success of those who have emerged from it.

The TC must remain available for the most motivated, while detoxification is needed for the 5 percent who never go back to heroin after a course particularly since it is rapid and less costly. MM attracts addicts who feel they cannot manage without the crutch of an opiate for a while. The other modalities to be described fit other needs and temperaments.

4 Narcotic Antagonists Methadone treatment has the disadvantage of maintaining the addiction to a narcotic. The narcotic antagonists are not narcotics, but have a chemical structure similar to that of the narcotics, so similar that it fools the nerve cell and occupies the binding sites that the heroin would have occupied to exert its effect. When all narcotic binding sites are filled with antagonist molecules, an injection of heroin will produce no high, and eventually the addict learns that it does no good to shoot heroin. Such treatment would seem ideal, but certain problems exist. Until recently the antagonists were too short-acting. Long-acting antagonists are now available. Large numbers of addicts who entered treatment dropped out because the antagonist did nothing to make them feel better. In contrast, methadone treatment seems to provide tranquilization. if not a high. It is likely that certain kinds of addicts will chose to be treated with the antagonists. but it will not become the most popular of treatments.

5 Religious Groups A number of religious or quasi-religious organizations have attempted to help the addict. Teen Challenge, Narcanon, Transcendental Meditation, and others are directly involved in rescuing drug abusers. Their claims of success are encouraging, but careful followup for extended periods of time is not available. The spiritual approach is attractive for those who hope to find meaning within or outside the self.

6 Traditional Therapies The use of supportive services counseling, group psychotherapy, vocational guidance. family therapy and others has been helpful for some addicted persons. Involuntary treatment of hard core criminal offenders is practiced in a few states. The incarceration of felony addicts as a means of getting them off the street does not produce more than abstinence while in jail if that. Individual psychotherapy can help only a selected handful of the addicted.

7 Heroin Maintenance The "British system' provides narcotics to proven addicts after an effort to rehabilitate them has been rejected. What is not realized in this country is that most English addicts receive methadone. Heroin is given only if methadone is refused. It is superficial to believe that we can solve our heroin problem by supplying all addicts with free, pure heroin. England has not solved its small problem with legal heroin, and ours, 200 times greater. is far more complex. For example, Britain has a minor, though growing black market while ours is very large and well established. Also the introduction of copious supplies of legal heroin would not lead to the disappearance of the narcotic syndicates; in fact. the illicit heroin might simply go into creating new consumer markets. Heroin maintenance is unavailable anywhere in the United States, and it is most unlikely that it will become permissible to use the procedure except in small. well-controlled experiments.

8 Control of Supplies Even with better treatment methods than we now have new addicts will continue to be made unless supplies are eliminated or greatly diminished. There can be no narcotic addicts without narcotics; even making the material difficult to obtain will reduce the demand. Therefore treatment efforts must be accompanied by control efforts. The analogy to epidemic spread is applicable here: treatment takes care of the carriers, control removes the cause of the epidemic. Since neither element can be completely successful, both are needed.

Who Is An Addict?

It is not always easy to determine who is addicted to heroin. At times nonaddicted individuals will present themselves to methadone clinics for treatment. It is a great responsibility to give someone a narcotic like methadone for years, and therefore the determination of the applicant's status is of great importance. The following signs are usually sought for as supportive evidence.

1 "Tracks" or discolorations along a vein from many old injections.
2 Needle marks from recent injections.
3 Proof of prior addiction from police, hospital, or other treatment records.
4 Urine testing for morphine. Such tests will establish only the presence of the narcotic in the system, not chronic use. Urine tests can also find barbiturates, amphetamines, cocaine, methadone, and other drugs.
5 Nalline testing. In a person who has taken narcotics during the past day, a small amount of Nalline, a narcotic antagonist, will cause contracted pupils to dilate. This signifies a recent narcotic intake, not addiction.
6 Abstinence symptoms. A person who claims to be an active addict should start developing abstinence symptoms (tearing, runny nose, gooseflesh, etc.) if kept under observation for 8 to 12 hours. These symptoms can be precipitated immediately by a small dose of Nalline, Narcan, Lorfan, or some other narcotic antagonist.

The Sedatives
and Tranquilizers

SEDATIVES

The procurement of quietude and sleep has been sought after since the cavemen. Many plants and chemicals have been found or developed to provide for a relaxation of the tensions of the day and for nocturnal sleep. Other medical uses of the sedatives include the management of convulsive seizures, as an anesthetic for minor operations, as a "truth" serum in psychiatry, and in small doses for a variety of psychosomatic disorders. The prototype of the sedatives is the barbiturates although nonbarbiturate sedatives are both used and abused. We are now into a change in style of drug abuse. The "downers" recently have become popular in contrast to the psychedelics and the stimulants of a decade ago. The depressants of mental functioning like sedatives, tranquilizers, narcotics, and alcohol are increasingly abused. The search seems to be for "awayness" and oblivion rather than alertness and awareness.

Most Frequently Abused Sedative Tranquilizers

Trade name	Generic name	Street name	Abuse potential
1 *Barbiturate sedatives*			
Seconal	secobarbital	reds	high
Nembutal	pentobarbital	yellow jackets	high
Amytal	amobarbital	blue angels	high
Tuinal	amobarbital-secobarbital	tuies	high
Luminal	phenobarbital	–	low
2 *Nonbarbiturate sedatives*			
Doriden	glutethimide	Cibas	high
Quaalude, Sopor	methaqualone	sopors	high
Chloral, Noctec	chloral hydrate	–	low
3 *Tranquilizers*			
Miltown, Equinal	meprobamate	–	low
Librium	chlordiazepoxide	–	low
Valium	diazepam	–	low

Polydrug Abuse

Another change in drug styles is polydrug use. Instead of a single drug of abuse, it is more common to find that many classes of agents are taken simultaneously or in sequence. The basic intoxicants are usually alcohol and marihuana; to them are added "downers," "uppers," hallucinogens, and narcotics in bewildering combinations. Combinations of depressants are particularly problematic, for they potentiate each other's action and depress the respiratory center. Alcohol and barbiturates are a frequent combination. Combining two sedatives can produce unexpected degrees of intoxication and stupor. It is by no means uncommon to find that a person who has died of an overdose has less than lethal amounts of alcohol and barbiturates in his or her blood. Of course, suicide is a possibility, but often enough, death is accidental, the deceased merely having drunk too much and having taken a number of sleeping pills to get a good night's rest.

Combined sedative-stimulant abuse is well known. These opposite-acting drugs do not cancel each other out, instead they smooth out the jitteriness that some note with stimulants. Dexamyl (purple hearts) is a dexedrine-amytal combination which is well thought of, but other combinations are also ingested. The combined use of heroin and cocaine, the "speedball," may be the original upper-downer, and it is still around. When addicts have difficulties obtaining heroin, they resort to almost anything else, usually one of the depressants. The polydrug user *par excellence* will take anything and everything, known and unknown.

Physiologic and Psychologic Effects

It would be imagined that a person taking large amounts of sedatives would go to sleep. This is not so in the tolerant individual, who may not only remain awake and stagger about, but may even be overactive and aggressive. Next to alcohol, the sedatives account for more violent acting-out than any other class of drugs. The picture of sleeping pill intoxication is identical to that of alcohol: incoordination, slurred speech, confusion, impaired judgement, and poor psychomotor performance. In higher doses the mental confusion increases and disorientation, hallucinations, and paranoid delusions develop.

Tolerance builds up within a few weeks, and amounts that would ordinarily produce death may be taken a number of times a day. The withdrawal state from large quantities of barbiturates is a serious medical emergency requiring hospitalization. It is identical to the alcoholic delirium tremens (DTs). After two or three days of abstinence, tremulousness, fever, rapid pulse, terrifying hallucinations, and major convulsions are encountered. As with the alcoholic DTs, death is a possibility in run-down patients. Nondrinkers who develop the DTs should be suspected of being in a sedative withdrawal state. The treatment consists of a very gradual reduction of the dose over many days or weeks.

Another danger to barbiturate addicts is their accident proneness. They are clumsy, impulsive, exercise poor judgement and have little insight into their impaired functioning. Barbiturates are among the most frequently used instruments for suicidal purposes, and the most common mode of self-destruction by women. A nontolerant person who takes 8 to 10 capsules or more may die, and 30 capsules would invariably be fatal. Death is due to respiratory arrest. Treatment includes support of breathing and heart function. Mouth-to-mouth breathing assistance, cardiac massage, oxygen, and more complicated measures may be required for recovery. The treatment of the chronic barbiturate addict, like that of the chronic alcoholic, is difficult and often not rewarding. After such addicts have been detoxified from sedatives, their anxiety should be treated with nonaddicting drugs or with nondrug techniques such as relaxing exercises and biofeedback measures.

If marihuana is predominantly a youth drug, and alcohol represents the standard potion of the older abuser, the generation gap is obliterated in sedative-tranquilizer abuse. Both young and old join together in their misuse of downers. Youngsters tend to find their supplies on the street, while aging adults look to prescriptions for their supplies. Tranquilizers used to be the exclusive domain of the middle-aged businessman or woman and of the housewife, but no longer. These items, too, have now been discovered by adolescents.

Quaalude

Quaalude requires special mention because of the recent widespread misuse of the drug. It was not that Quaalude represented a particularly novel or safe sedative, but the fact that it became easily available in large quantities, that accounted for its popularity. The side effects and complications are identical to those of other sedatives. The effects are quite similar, and differences are more likely to be due to promotional persuasion than to pharmacology. Withdrawal states and deaths have occurred. A number of false notions have been circulating with regard to Quaalude, and these can be quickly corrected. Quaalude is no safer than any other sleeping pill, and in combination with alcohol (luding out) can be hazardous. It is addicting in large amounts. It is not an aphrodisiac, although it has been touted as "heroin for lovers." What has been rediscovered by its consumers is the relaxation of ego controls that all depressants produce. This permits sexual activity which may not have occurred without the sedative. Sexual performance would be improved only if anxiety were interfering with sexual functioning; otherwise it would be impaired by the drug.

TRANQUILIZERS

An overlap between the class of sedatives and that of tranquilizers exists. Small doses of sedatives act as daytime relaxants, and tranquilizers can cause sleep. The tranquilizers are a relatively modern group of agents, and their primary actions are antianxiety, calming, and reducing tension. Two kinds of tranquilizers are identified: major and minor. The major tranquilizers are so called because they are used in the treatment of major psychiatric disturbances: psychoses like schizophrenia and mania. Thorazine, Stelazine, and Mellaril are examples of this group. They are almost never abused because they do not produce euphoria and have unpleasant side effects. In small doses they are also used to treat lesser conditions like anxiety. The minor tranquilizers are the classic antianxiety agents. They relax muscles, reduce aggressiveness, and have some anticonvulsant properties. Miltown, Librium, and Valium are examples of this subgroup. They have been taken in large amounts to obtain a high, but their abuse remains modest in comparison to the sedatives. One feature of all tranquilizers is their safety. Their lethal dose is far higher than their effective dose, in contrast to the sedatives where the lethal dose may be only 10 times higher than the average dose. Tolerance does occur with the minor tranquilizers, as well as cross-tolerance with sleeping pills and alcohol. A withdrawal syndrome develops if a person has been using very large amounts for months, and then stops.

Chapter 8

The Volatile Solvents and Other Anesthetics

General Anesthetics

It is noteworthy that all three of the early general anesthetics—ether, chloroform, and nitrous oxide were used as recreational intoxicating agents even before their medical benefits were recognized. In the nineteenth century, as noted earlier, chloroform parties were held at Cambridge University and elsewhere. The safer ether was more widespread as a source of fun. Ether frolics were well known among the students at Harvard and lesser schools. Because of the tax on alcohol, either threatened to displace it in some countries, for example, mid-eighteenth century Ireland. The intoxication was briefer, and the hangover less troublesome so that one could get drunk a number of times a day. Effective techniques were developed for swallowing ether so that it did not burn on the way down.

Nitrous oxide (laughing gas) was the nineteenth century psychedelic. College students, writers, high society, and anyone willing to spend a quarter at a county fair laughing gas exhibition could discover the hilarious and delightful inebriation. This mundane anesthetic, now administered for dental extractions, has relevance to the current scene. Some descriptions of its effects rival today's psychedelic reports. William James called nitrous oxide a mind-expanding experience. Many have been impressed by the nitrous oxide state, during which they achieved enormous philosophic truths and insights, while at the same time getting rid of a carious tooth. At present an occasional laughing gas sniffer turns up. It is used not only in hospitals, but also as a whipped cream propellent and in certain industrial processes. An occasional theft from a hospital supply house or industrial supplier has been recorded. Other anesthetics, ketamine, for example, share this interesting property of self-dissociation in the interval between waking and sleeping. Carbon dioxide inhalations do something quite similar.

Volatile Solvents

The inhalation of organic solvents, which are related to the anesthetics, is still another method to achieve intoxication. While solvents are not highly thought of among the connoisseurs of consciousness manipulation, their use persists year after year. Often they are the first abused substances, and underprivileged male juveniles are their clientele. These juveniles seem attracted to volatile solvents because they are inexpensive, and because no stockpile of alcoholic beverages to be sampled exists in the home. The main products would include airplane glue, paint thinner, gasoline, any of the aerosols, and a wide variety of other household and commercial fluids. Even if the solvent contains toxic material such as an insecticide or metallic paint, it will be sniffed by someone. The material is ordinarily poured into a plastic bag or on a rag and inhaled or sniffed. The practice is usually solitary although glue parties are known.

The resulting picture is one of a delirium. Confusion, impaired thinking, emotional loosening, and clumsiness are to be observed. The user may mention dizziness, drowsiness, a dreamy "high," and a hallucination or two. Speech is slurred and a period of excitement may intervene during which injuries can be incurred. Sleep is a frequent end point. The intoxication lasts only minutes, at most an hour or two.

A partial tolerance to the fumes develops with daily use. Other depressants potentiate the action, and wine is sometimes drunk to increase the effect. A withdrawal state has not been reported although the habit is not always easy to break. A chronic cough and a rash around the nose and mouth are not infrequent. Claims that liver, kidney, bone marrow, and brain damage occur cannot be accurately assessed since a thorough study of this problem has not yet been undertaken. Accidents certainly happen, and poisoning from the solvent itself or from the material dissolved in it has been documented. One form of death from aerosol sniffing is cardiac arrest and over 100 such cases have been collected. Death has also occurred from asphyxiation when youngsters have sniffed solvents in enclosed spaces such as plastic bags. Gasoline sniffing, which appears to be increasing at present, may be associated with lead poisoning. Gasoline may be the only intoxicant available to the poor rural young. Most sniffers grow out of their habit; unfortunately they generally shift over to alcohol or barbiturate abuse.

Those who have studied groups of solvent users generally find a disorganized family and social situation, peers who are involved in similar practices, and delinquent behavior on the part of the individual.

Although nonintoxicating and repellent model airplane glues have been marketed, the solution to solvent abuse can hardly be achieved by such means. Volatile solvents are simply too pervasive. Educating children to develop their own internal controls, devising more satisfactory after-school activities, working with gangs and the family are some possible rational approaches. Anything that can be done to increase a youngster's confidence and self-respect, and to help him deal with the problems of everyday life, will wean him from the need for evading life through solvents.

Amyl Nitrite A volatile liquid that has a peculiar form of aberrant usage is amyl nitrite ("poppers"). Amyl nitrite is manufactured in ampules covered with a nylon net so that they can be safely and quickly broken and the contents inhaled in instances of coronary spasm (angina pectoris). The substance dilates blood vessels and relieves the chest pain associated with angina. It also dilates the blood vessels in the brain, and a few doctors, nurses, and other knowledgeable people inhale poppers prior to orgasm to prolong and intensify the sensation. Except for an occasional headache and dizziness, adverse effects have not been found.

Chapter 9

Alcohol, a Dangerous Drug

Pharmacology

It is difficult to think of an alcoholic beverage as a drug in this culture, but it is one and a dangerous one for many millions of people. Alcohol is also a food, but one that is a poor source of calories since it provides no vitamins, and in fact, requires factors in the B-complex for its own metabolism. It is the diminished vitamin intake and increased vitamin demand of persons who obtain a major fraction of their calories from alcohol that account for some of the complications of prolonged use. Other deleterious effects are caused by the toxic effect of alcohol itself upon body cells.

Alcohol is an anesthetic, the most ancient one of all. In low doses it may appear to stimulate, but in increasing amounts a progressive depression of brain function develops. Almost all the alcohol ingested is oxidized in a series of complex steps via acetaldehyde and acetate to water and carbon dioxide. The metabolic breakdown is fairly constant for each person and averages approximately the amount in a cocktail per hour. Larger amounts accumulate and produce the characteristic signs of intoxication. A blood alcohol concentration of 0.1 percent (100 mg in 100cc) or more is the usual level of legal intoxication. It is achieved by swallowing about three drinks within a short period on an empty stomach. An impairment in the performance of skilled tasks can be detected with even lower levels. At 0.2 percent moderate intoxication is evident. At 0.3 percent intoxication is marked, and at 0.4 percent the person is comatose. Death can occur at blood levels beyond 0.5 percent.

Causes of Alcoholism

Drinking that causes physical or mental harm to drinkers, or seriously impairs them socially, economically, or in their relations with others can be considered problem drinking. Alcoholism or alcohol addiction emphasizes the psychological and physical dependence on the substance. There is no single cause of alcoholism. Instead, alcoholism results from a complex interaction of factors as outlined below.

Psychologic Factors Many, but by no means all, alcoholics are passive dependent individuals with a low tolerance for life stress. Alcohol reduces their tension, allows them to avoid their problems, and permits them to be dependent and require care. In a way they are treating their emotional inadequacies with drink.

Sociocultural Factors It is easier to become an alcoholic in some societies or subgroups within societies than in others. Contributing factors include early learned attitudes, parental role models, peer drinking activities, the degree of social deprivation, and the pressures to imbibe within the group.

Constitutional Factors Some individuals appear to have been born with a vulnerability to drink in excess. This is not, however, a specific inherited quality; instead it may stem from a diminished ability to cope with stress. It has been said that alcoholism is a disease, a metabolic disorder. Although prolonged drinking can result in severe metabolic disorders, a metabolic cause has yet to be found.

Over 80 percent of Americans over fifteen years of age have used alcoholic beverages, and a large majority continue to do so without apparent harm. It is true that even socially consumed amounts of alcohol are thought to be harmful by some experts. They speak of the "myth of social drinking" and indicate that evidence exists of injurious effects upon various organs. Some cell injury may be due to "sludging," or clumping of red blood cells in the smallest blood vessels. Small amounts of alcohol have been demonstrated to increase sludging. Longevity statistics have shown that drinkers of moderate amounts of spirits live as long as abstainers.

If the effects of small amounts of alcohol were not pleasant, it could hardly have become the universal recreational drug that it is. In moderate amounts, feelings of relaxation and a mild euphoria are detectable.

What constitutes moderate drinking? A nineteenth century English physician's definition remains reasonable to this day. No more than two mixed drinks (or two 12-ounce bottles of beer or two wine glasses of unfortified wine) in 24 hours is considered moderate usage. That amount should be taken with food and cannot be saved up to expend on some subsequent occasion. However, even two drinks are too much for certain people like recovered alcoholics, diabetics, or epileptics who should never drink at all.

Adolescent Alcoholism

Almost every school survey indicates that alcohol and tobacco are the first and most frequently used drugs among adolescents.[1] Any theory that assumes that certain young people escalate from less harmful drugs to more dangerous ones like heroin must account for the fact that alcohol is the first intoxicant to be used. Even among young adults who sneered at the Establishment intoxicant a few years ago, a movement back to the "pop" wines and other beverages is evident. Whether it is used alone or in combination with other more exotic chemicals, the rediscovery of alcohol provides an interesting illustration of the fact that the more things change, the more they remain the same.

Excessive drinking has been found in certain urban grade school students. Among seventh-graders, 63 percent of boys and 54 percent of girls had tried alcoholic beverages. By the twelfth grade this increased to 93 and 87 percent respectively. Of these, between 5 and 10 percent

[1]*Alcohol and Health*, Second Special Report to the U.S. Congress, U.S. Government Printing Office, Washington, D.C., 1974, pp. 8–12.

were developing excessive drinking patterns. Increasing numbers of teen-agers and persons in their twenties are being seen in AA groups, and the age at which cirrhosis of the liver is being diagnosed is dropping. Since cirrhosis develops only after years of heavy drinking, it is clear that adolescent alcoholism is a growing problem. It appears that youth are no wiser than their elders in moderating their consumption of alcohol.

Another interesting development in teenage drinking patterns is evolving as states lower the legal age limit for the purchase and public use of alcohol to 18. This is the disturbing increase in the incidence of fatal traffic accidents involving the 18 to 21 age group that has been reported where alcohol is detected in the blood of the drivers.

It is the peer group much more than the family unit that deter-mines whether the adolescent will drink, and whether he will drink intemperately. Being drunk is perceived by many young people as a way to seem grown up. Drinking to excess becomes a pattern of prestige. Unfortunately, nothing in adult social behavior or in the mass media contradicts this erroneous notion. Drinking patterns of a lifetime are sometimes established during adolescence.

Personal and Social Costs of Alcohol

1 Ten million people including increasing numbers of teenagers are now dependent upon alcohol in this country, and their use of it is out of control. This means that some 40 million people (the afflicted and their families) are directly suffering from the results of prolonged, excessive drinking.

2 Alcohol is the drug that provokes violent behavior more fre-quently than any other. In 90 percent of all assaults, and 50 to 60 percent of all rapes and homicides, the aggressors were found to be under the influence.

3 Police statistics across the nation reveal that a third to a half of all arrests are alcohol-related.

4 The fact that alcoholic beverages produce a rather lengthy period of intoxication means that for many hours judgement is im-paired, control over behavior is diminished, and motor skills are reduced. This leads to an accident-prone state during which both drinkers and persons in their vicinity are at risk. To cite only one aspect of this problem, about 800,000 traffic accidents a year are ascribed to drunk drivers or pedestrians. Over 25,000 people die each year from these accidents.

5   The failure of controls over one's behavior, and the depression that can become overt during drinking, are reasons why the suicide rate among alcoholics has been found to be 6 to 20 times higher than in the general population in various studies.[2]

6   Alcohol has been a major disrupter of family life. It has been found that 60 percent of marriages in which one or both partners are alcohol-dependent, will end in divorce or separation. Children of parents who drink excessively are affected by neglect, persecution, and physical attacks upon them. As a result of their disorganized childhood, 55 percent become alcoholics themselves.[3]

7   The total economic loss to government, industry and other sectors of society is now placed at 25 billion a year.

8   Chronic alcoholism causes brain damage, nerve damage, liver damage, and pancreas damage. Cirrhosis of the liver is now the fourth leading cause of death among males fifty-five to sixty-five years of age. Resistance to infection is impaired, and pneumonia and tuberculosis are well known among heavy drinkers. The life span of the chronic user is shortened by 11 years. Recently, alcoholic addicts have been found to sustain higher than average rates of cancer of the liver, throat, and upper gastrointestinal tract.

9   A fifth to a quarter of all admissions to psychiatric hospitals are for acute or chronic alcoholism.

10   Alcohol produces a true addiction. Heavy drinking induces tolerance, craving, and a withdrawal state called the DTs. The delirium tremens is a frightening and occasionally lethal withdrawal state; it deters only a very few from subsequent ethanol (alcohol) intake.

11   A major problem in treating problem alcoholics is their refusal to see themselves as more than social drinkers. They will tend to deny that their drinking is out of control despite obvious evidence to the contrary.

12   Despite heated debates about one drug or another being a steppingstone to heroin, in every survey alcohol is found to be the first intoxicating drug used by adolescents. But such discussions are pointless because young persons dependent upon alcohol are in just as much trouble as if they were dependent on heroin.

It is obvious that we badly need new cultural attitudes toward excessive drinking. The costs of alcoholism are becoming too onerous. We must come to understand that it is not only a drug, but a dangerous

[2] D. W. Goodwin, "Alcohol in Suicide and Homicide," *Quart. J. Studies Alcohol*, 34: 144, 1973.
[3] R. M. Bennett et al., "Alcohol and Human Physical Aggression, *Quart. J. Studies Alcohol*, 30: 870, 1969.

drug for millions. If it were to come up at present for legalization as a newly discovered recreational drug, it would never be acceptable to lawmakers and their health advisors because of its many adverse effects.

Effects of Alcohol

Alcohol progressively depresses brain cell functioning, beginning with the highest cerebral centers and ending in the brain stem. Even the initial feeling of stimulation and euphoria is due to a depression of the controls normally maintained over thinking, emotion, and behavior. Thinking becomes loosened, judgement less reliable, emotions more labile, and behavior less controlled. The cerebellar locomotion centers are affected producing problems with coordination of movement and speech. With increasing amounts, drowsiness, stupor, and coma intervene. The center in the medulla that controls breathing finally becomes sufficiently depressed, and respirations stop.

When heavy drinking continues over long periods, a number of changes occur in various organs, which can lead to difficulties. Alcohol is a stimulator of stomach secretions. Eventually, the stomach lining becomes inflamed, a condition called alcoholic gastritis. The gastritis, or the peptic ulcer that is sometimes associated with it, can bleed profusely. Bleeding is a real hazard for alcoholics because their dietary intake is poor, and the proteins and vitamins needed to form coagulating factors are missing. Furthermore, the iron and other nutrients required to build red blood cells are in short supply. A severely damaged liver adds to the bleeding proclivity by not being able to manufacture clotting factors, and by producing a block to the flow of blood resulting in fragile, easily ruptured varicose veins in the stomach and esophagus.

Large amounts of alcohol produce an enlarged, fatty liver. Inflammation of the liver (alcoholic hepatitis) can lead to liver cell death. The resulting scarring of the liver is called cirrhosis. Cirrhosis, which is associated with nausea, loss of appetite, abdominal distress, and jaundice, is developed by about a quarter of all alcoholics. Alcoholics who eat well seem to be partially protected. Inflammation of the pancreas follows prolonged alcohol abuse, and is a further cause of abdominal pain and diabetes in drinkers.

The nerves of the extremities can be paralyzed by alcohol in large amounts. Numbness, tingling, and weakness of the arms and legs result. A number of mental conditions occur in connection with chronic inebriation some of which are irreversible and require custodial care. Alcoholics can come down with beri beri—a heart disease due to insufficient vitamin B1. Alcohol is also directly toxic to the heart muscle cell in sufficient concentrations over long periods.

Prevention

It is difficult to believe that destructive drinking can be prevented or even decreased in a society that overtly and covertly encourages its use to excess. In fact, prevention efforts have not been successful up to now. Prohibition has failed, slick slogans have failed, educational efforts based upon the dangers of alcohol have failed. The National Institute on Alcohol Abuse and Alcoholism suggests the following directions and emphases for prevention:

1 It must be recognized that alcohol is a socially available agent used by the majority, and that efforts to remove it have failed.

2 In cultures that experience minimal problems in connection with drinking, alcohol is used early in life in a family or religious setting.

3 Patterns of alcohol usage exist that do not result in problems with the substance. This country must attempt to achieve such patterns.

4 Physical, emotional, and social distrubances should not be self-treated with alcohol in the search for relief. In fact, the use of alcohol over time for such purposes is counterproductive.

5 In a society that tolerates drunkenness as an acceptable aspect of drinking behavior, a high incidence of alcoholism must be expected.

To change the current patterns, children should learn healthy attitudes about drinking in their homes. Schools should teach information about alcohol use, reinforcing the responsible use of alcohol with food, and stress that intoxication is sickness and not manliness. Encouraging such attitudes in the home and the school may help reduce the number of problem drinkers.

Help For the Alcoholic

Detoxification (drying out) consists of assisting the person who has been on a binge, or who has been drinking steadily, to achieve an alcohol-free state. Anxiety and sleeplessness are invariably present. Impending DTs mark the beginning of the withdrawal syndrome. Tremulousness, sweating, a low fever, nausea, and restlessness are the early symptoms of delirium tremens. With adequate treatment the more severe manifestations, convulsions and delirium, may be avoided. Any depressant—alcohol, barbiturates, or tranquilizers—can be used to provide sedation. Nutritious food, fluids, vitamins, and minerals are needed to replenish a depleted patient. Simply drying out someone is a futile exercise, since relapse is common. Instead, this period must be exploited to start the rehabilitative process and to make specific plans for abstinence. Drugs used for detoxification are phased out slowly, and attention is paid to the client's social and personal problems.

Alcoholics Anonymous (AA) is a lay organization of alcoholics in various phases of recovery. They meet and mutually support each other in their efforts to stop drinking. Two basic conditions must be met for involvement in the program. The first is the admission that one has lost the ability to manage one's life. The second is the turning over of one's life to a higher power. The AA meeting is a key component of the program, but person-to-person assistance is also thought to be important. AA success rate is said to be 60 to 75 percent. This is difficult to confirm since no records or statistics are kept in order to maintain anonymity.

Psychotherapy is needed for some alcoholics with serious personality problems. Group therapy is ordinarily preferred to individual treatment for many reasons. Alcoholics may resent being placed in a patient-therapist relationship, and will not enter a situation that they see as a threat to their idea of themselves. They may prefer the nonauthoritarian setting of a group in which everyone has a similar problem. The group provides a training ground for identifying interpersonal difficulties and for working them through. It can also provide the example of alcoholics who have progressed successfully in dealing with their problems, thus offering the newcomers hope that they can do it, too.

Antabuse (tetraethylthiuram disulfide) is a chemical which blocks the enzymatic breakdown of acetaldehyde. Acetaldehyde accumulates in the body and causes a number of unpleasant effects including flushing, vomiting, headache, faintness, and weakness. Alcohol consumed while Antabuse is in the body will usually induce a feeling of being sick. Persons on Antabuse know that if they drink, they will get sick, and the Antabuse therefore serves as a deterrent.

Other treatments include hypnosis, LSD, antianxiety or antidepressive drugs, religious fellowships, and counseling services. The essential element of all rehabilitation efforts is reeducation, so that the individual can learn new methods of dealing with life's difficulties, and new ways of structuring his life so that drinking is no longer needed or desired.

Chapter 10

Deliriants, Old and New

The hallmark of a delirium (also called a toxic psychosis) is mental confusion. Consciousness is clouded, and the ability to think may be so impaired that disorientation occurs. First, a loss of time orientation takes place. The day, the month, or the year may not be correctly recalled. The city or country may be falsely identified. Finally one's name could even be forgotten. Many drugs already mentioned can cause a delirium. Alcohol, the solvents, and the sedatives are representative. In fact, any drug in overdose can distort brain metabolism sufficiently to produce a toxic psychosis. Certain drugs produce an allergic response in certain people even in small amounts, and the brain can be involved in the reaction. Nonchemical stress on the brain cells can induce a confusional state. Fever, overexposure to the sun, serious kidney or liver disease, and head injuries are some other causes of delirial states. The change in consciousness produced by schizophrenia or ordinary amounts of LSD should not be called a delirium. Substantial alterations of awareness do take place, but true confusion is rarely present.

A number of occasionally abused drugs will be discussed here which do not easily fall into the categories mentioned in previous chapters. They produce the intoxicated state mentioned above with some regularity.

Belladonna (*Atropa belladonna*) is called deadly nightshade in the folklore. It has a long and variable history. Professional poisoners depended on it long before the Borgias employed it in their repertoire of poisons. Women made themselves more beautiful by dilating their pupils with a drop of the tincture in each eye. Small amounts were allegedly put into the wine during bacchanalias to intensity the inebriated revelry, and to loosen controls over behavior. Atropine is the major alkaloid of Belladonna, and its current uses are far less exotic than those of bygone days. It is used to dilate the pupil prior to eye examinations, and it is found in medication for stomach ulcers. Only rarely is it deliberately misused because the side effects are unpleasant.

Datura stramonium has many common names. It is called Jamestown or Jimson weed (from Jamestown, Virginia) stinkweed, thorn apple, and devil's-apple. It contains atropine and hyocine, and it was well known to the sorcerers and witches of yore. Datura was a main ingredient of the brew mixed for the infamous witches' Sabbath ritual, during which all manner of actual and hallucinated goings-on took place. The American Indians knew Jimson weed well, and some of the tribes employed it as an ordeal in rites to initiate their young men into manhood. Pre-Columbian Indians are said to have given Datura to the slaves and wives of their dead masters to put them into a drunken stupor before buying them alive with the deceased. A platoon of Redcoats who had been sent down to Jamestown to subdue Nathaniel Bacon's rebellion against the British gathered some Jimson leaves and used it as a green in a salad. They sustained a curious 10-day episode of hilarious madness, which rendered them quite ineffective. The same common poisonous weed still is heard from today. Experimenting schoolboys in Ventura County, California, have tried the leaves and managed to intoxicate themselves. Their dilated pupils, flushed faces, dry mouths, galloping pulses, and florid deliria reproduced a 2,000 year-old syndrome. *Asthmador* is an old-fashioned asthma "cure" that contains belladonna and datura among other herbs. It can be purchased without a prescription in some states. A few exploring young people discovered that one can go out of one's mind by swallowing large amounts of Asthmador. The effectiveness of this asthma remedy is in doubt, and the wisdom of its sale over-the-counter without controls is dubious. However, datura grows wild in many places, and it will have a future as well as a past.

Henbane belongs to the same family as belladonna and datura. It is a bane, not only to hens, but also to humans. Its official name is *Hyocyamus niger* and it contains scopolamine. In ancient days it was secretly given to a victim to cast a spell over him. He routinely related that he saw demons and believed he was in Hell—the precursor of today's "bum trip." Nor is it necessary to swallow henbane; an ointment of it rubbed on the skin induces a frenzied, nightmarish delirium. Scopolamine, its alkaloid, had a short period of popularity as a "truth serum" and also as a means of inducing a twilight sleep in obstetrical patients during childbirth. It is found in tiny amounts in some sleeping pills sold over the counter. On rare occasions a youngster is brought into an emergency room after having taken the entire contents of a box of patent medicine for sleep.

Mandrake (*Mandragora officinarum*) was used as a truth drug by the Chinese emperors long before the Christian era. After the criminal had confessed, mandrake wine also served to numb the pain of his death on the rack. Roman soldiers gave it to those about to be crucified to benumb the senses. Professional poisoners made use of it during the Middle Ages. Mandrake is mentioned in the Old Testament as a fertility potion. No doubt, the forked root that resembles the human limbs is the major basis for that belief. Mandrake was sold in most love philtres in the days when such stimulators of sex were needed. Specially qualified mandrake witchwives were selected to collect the root because it was supposed to provoke unearthly shrieking while being pulled out— shrieks so appalling that anyone hearing them went insane. Only an isolated instance of current misuse of mandrake is reported.

The *nutmeg tree* (*Myristica fragrans*) provides us with nutmeg and mace, spices which can produce a crude delirium in tablespoon amounts. In certain prisons the abuse of these cooking flavorings is sufficiently well known that they are kept locked up. Two to six nutmegs (one half to one ounce) can result in a delirium with hallucinations and eventually a drugged sleep. The effects are generally delayed for hours, but the intoxication can last for days. In large amounts many unpleasant side effects are evident: cramps, headache, weak pulse, dizziness, chest pain, and even collapse. Some patients complain of extreme thirst and considerable apprehension. A century ago it was believed that nutmeg could induce an abortion. Women who took large quantities became so toxic they sometimes did abort.

The *fly agaric* (*Amanita muscarina*) is the red spotted mushroom that Walt Disney popularized in his movie *Fantasia*. Its use as an intoxicant goes back to prehistory. It may have been Soma, so highly praised in the Vedas. It "made men like Gods" according to that ancient legend. Before vodka displaced it, the Koryak tribesmen of Kamchatka used it as their intoxicant. It is one of the few mind-altering substances that is eliminated unchanged. How the Koryaks discovered this pharmacologic fact is unknown, but Oliver Goldsmith and others have reported the practice of drinking the urine of agaric eaters to share in the "high." Apparently the chemistry of the fly agaric (so called because medieval housewives killed flies by placing the mushroom pieces in a dish of water) has changed over the centuries since the Vedas were written. Nowadays, eating the Amanita produces unpleasant symptoms and a rather confused mental state.

There is no end to the search for novel intoxicants. A few years ago it was dried banana peel scrapings—a harmless and ineffective material. Those who got stoned on "mellow yellow," as the cigarettes were called, demonstrated once again how suggestible we humans are. New pseudo-psychedelic concoctions come forth from the drug-using subculture: try baby woodrose seeds, smoke spider webs, eat spoiled wheat germ, swallow rotten green pappers, chew Scotch broom, mainline mayonnaise. Considering the problems that confront us, what we need least of all are new ways to become delirious.

Chapter 11

The "Head"

In this society almost every young person will have tried a mind-altering drug at one time, especially if alcohol is included. Why is it that some experiment and stop using, others continue to indulge at spaced intervals, and a small number will make it a way of life? Studies of marihuana users found that those who used marihuana very few times, or who use it only on special social occasions, could not be differentiated on personality testing from nonusers. It was the daily, regular user, the "pothead," who showed up as a more emotionally disturbed individual. Similar results have been obtained in comparisons of large numbers of young people who drink either not at all, slightly, socially, and excessively. Actually, it does not matter too much which chemical is abused; when it becomes a way of life the dangers multiply. So it is the "head," whether a "rumhead," a "pothead," a "pillhead," a "hophead," or an "acidhead," who is at greatest risk. If physical or mental complications occur, the head is most likely to be afflicted. There is a further hazard: when some drug becomes the sole mechanism by which the stresses and the frustrations of life are handled, a sort of maturation arrest takes place. If techniques of dealing with problems are not learned. psychological growth stops. The goal is not to evade the difficulties of everyday existence, but to learn ways to cope with and solve them. If this is not learned, chemical escape becomes the only option available.

Many people try drugs, most of them step away after a brief or a longer exposure. There is something special about those who stay committed. They are usually in psychological pain, and the drug gives them a greater degree of relief than others obtain. The reason for taking a mind-changing drug can, in a gross and oversimplified way, be expressed as: "to feel better." It may be to assuage inner distress, or it may simply be to feel better than one does. If someone is in considerable distress, the relief will be that much greater. A "cure" has been found for the hurt and is not likely to be given up easily. What kind of people have, and what kind of situations induce the greatest psychic pain. They can be listed, and they represent the greatest risk factors for the induction of drug dependency.

PSYCHOSOCIAL FACTORS

1 Those with serious personality defects are predisposed. Inadequate, immature, emotionally unstable individuals with low tolerance to frustration have been labelled "addictive personalities." They surely are overrepresented when groups of addicts are examined. Very depressed and anxious people are also vulnerable. The borderline psychotic and the schizophrenic hope to become "more like people" and seek some chemical magic to produce that change.

2 Psychopaths are overrepresented among addict populations. Their internal controls are attenuated, and anything that they can get away with goes. Gratification of drives is not to be delayed. Overinvolvement with drugs is only one manifestation of their delinquent activities.

3 People who are unable to enjoy sober existence find in drugs the pleasure they cannot otherwise achieve. The inability to enjoy may be intrinsic, or their life situation may be dismal—or they may believe it to be. Chemical joy becomes the waking mode.

4 Curiosity is often given as a reason for drug usage especially among young people. The normal exploratory behavior of adolescents certainly can lead to sampling various chemicals. But curiosity will

rarely sustain a habit unless the person becomes locked into it through the physical dependence bind.

5 Boredom is another word often heard when causes of drug dependence are discussed. People will go to great lengths to avoid boredom. Boredom is as noxious as anxiety and frustration, and escape is eagerly sought. The chemical experience is one way out. A career as a head may be entered mainly because there is nothing better to do.

6 Man is a mimicking animal, and if others are doing something, that, in itself, is reason enough to do likewise. If one's group is involved, taking drugs is necessary, or else there is nothing else to do or talk about.

7 A head can be made accidentally. Almost any person in pain may be given narcotics unskillfully and wind up addicted. A friend might be turned onto one of the drugs that produce withdrawal symptoms if suddenly discontinued, and the habit might be perpetuated. Sometimes, not often, heads will hook younger persons out of malicious pleasure, to show them a good time, control them, or use them as a source of income.

8 Related to the preceding situation is the person who is persuaded or persuades himself to use an addicting substance. If a husband or boyfriend is already dependent on an opiate or alcohol, the wife or girlfriend often joins him. She may try to drink with him to help him, and often winds up a "junkie" or a "lush" herself.

9 Sometimes fairly stable people end up addicted. They may be in extremely stressful situations and have access to supplies. The classic example is the doctor or nurse who has to keep going beyond his or her endurance. Such persons discover that an injection of Demerol dissolves their fatigue. Businessmen fall into the same trap with alcohol, artists with cocaine.

10 Mention must be made of the "omnihead," the person who will imbibe or inject anything and everything. Some unbelievable concoctions are instilled into the body, some of them unintended for use by man or beast. Such "chuckwagon" consumers of chemicals are desperately depressed and prefer any existence or nonexistence to their current state.

11 Artists have traditionally been involved with drug experiences for a number of reasons. They are often in spiritual pain. Through an alteration of the state of consciousness they hope for a renewal of their creative powers, or for some sort of artistic breakthrough. They are always looking for new ways to fracture the ordinary perceptual set and to see or sense the world around them differently. Certain drugs help achieve this, and dependence is a danger.

12 Some people have become entranced with the drug experience because they discover great personal insights or have what seem to be religious experiences. Psychedelics is the group of drugs usually associated with these events, but opiates, alcohol, amphetamines, and cocaine sometimes provide similar experiences. Users seek new levels of awareness and the expansion of their ordinary consciousness. Perhaps some of these experiences have a validity. What is even more important is the working through of the insights, and the integration of the chemical transcendental state into daily conduct; without such integration the value of the experience disappears. But a person who has undergone such a profound moment may repetitively try again and again to achieve it and go beyond. He or she has not come to realize that the hard work of synthesizing these experiences must be completed first.

13 Observing chronic alcoholics and narcotic addicts who go through a marrow-shaking withdrawal, or who are rescued from death's door following an overdose or an infection, one anticipates that they would surely never start using again. Although "hitting bottom" may be a time to quit for some, most slip back to their old ways. The old conditioning is too strong, and neither the punishment they took, nor the life-endangering situation was a corrective behavioral experience.

14 The significance of the peer as an introducer into drug usage has been discussed. Peers also play a role in determining the severity of drug usage. Heads generate other heads.

Perhaps, if the life of the head were visualized as an effort at treatment of the psychosocial deficits that exist, his or her destructive career would be better understood. If he is a lonely, shy person, the drug provides confidence and an array of "friends" with a common bond. If she is bored, the life of the addict is full of the business of supporting the habit. Under the influence of the drugs the head feels adequate, imperturbable, *someone*. Disturbing sexual or aggressive drives that could hardly be inhibited in the past can now be readily expressed or repressed. If he is an angry young man, bitter at social injustice, he can defy authority as an addict without having to deal with complex social problems. If one's life situation is miserable with a disastrous family life, unspeakable squalor all around, and no apparent way out, the life of the "head" provides an easy escape from it all. Thus it "cures" all malignant personal, interpersonal, and transpersonal disruptions. Of course, nothing changes, nothing is learned, the injustices remain; in fact, things get worse underneath the superficial cure.

DRUG SPECIFICITY

Is a depressed person attracted to a life on stimulants? Do the anxious prefer "downers?" Although such preferences may exist, they are hardly invariable. Considering the variety of chemicals that some imbibe, the specific action seems less important then the blurring or erasure of ordinary awareness. An anesthetic like alcohol will do anything that the personality and the setting dictates: it will stimulate, depress, make amorous, garrulous, or aggressive, promote camaraderie or withdrawal. This should not imply that pharmacologic effects are insignificant. In the higher dosage ranges everyone becomes anesthetized on booze. It is at the lower dosage levels that the nondrug variables can decisively intervene.

The drug-personality-setting equation must include another factor if we are to understand the current situation. That factor is the general nature of the times. We are living through a period of enormous change, and rapid change causes stress. It is a period of vast upheaval of established values and attitudes, and of revolutionary alterations in our way of life. Young and old are suffering the effects of change. The old goals seem less appropriate; new and meaningful aspirations are not yet clearly discernible. Right and wrong are blurred, causes are unclear, and solutions appear remote or impossible. People feel helpless and dissatisfied, seeing the world as cruel, unjust, and decadent. It seems to many like the End. What is forgotten, or rather what has never been learned, is that man and society have gone through innumerable periods when the End appeared imminent. The cyclicity of history must be recognized, otherwise we are caught up in mistaking for catastrophe what is just a minor twist of the wheel. Furthermore, the notion that this is the worst of all possible worlds can easily be challenged by someone who has studied the past history of man. In fact, the opposite may be true. But the actual human condition does not matter. If people feel alienated and hopeless, they are. If the world is perceived as a place not worth living in, it is. We drop out—a practice of great antiquity. We become victims of our ignorance, anxieties, and lack of faith. Then, the bedrugged life seems preferable to what we are, or what we can struggle toward. Withdrawal by means of chemicals has great appeal. It is easy.

IDENTIFICATION OF THE USER

Early identification of a user of drugs is desirable both in order to help the user and to prevent the spread of the practice. Sometimes, sympathetic counseling prevents the progression to a head status. It is evident that the early signs of abuse are not easily recognized. Usually, more revealing than the direct effects of drug usage are the sudden changes in disposition and interest patterns. A different set of friends may appear, sleep might become a daytime activity, while the night is spent going out. Food intake can diminish, and dress and personal hygiene suffer. School attendance becomes irregular, study is neglected, and grades soon drop off. Drugs cost more than most allowances will buy. The need for money can become formidable if heroin or cocaine comes to be used regularly. Other drugs impose less of a financial strain, but even they result in frequent requests for money. Alternatively, money or salable household items may disappear, or the youngster may resort to shoplifting. The medicine chest may become depleted of a variety of items. The attitude toward family members often undergoes marked changes. Irritability, impatience, and anger reflect a loss of interest in family activities, and a preoccupation with the new life. These changes are not in themselves indicative of drug overuse, but they accompany it. They require a conversation with the young person, not an accusation.

When someone is seen under the influence of a drug the evidence may be negligible or marked. Drunken movements, speech, or thinking may or may not be present. The stimulants and hallucinogens dilate the pupils of the eyes, sometimes to the point where they will not react to light. The opiate user has pinpoint pupils even in a light room. Dark glasses may be worn to conceal these changes. The odor of marihuana, alcohol, and the solvents lingers on. Incense may be burned to mask it. The skin surface can be revealing. Fresh needle marks, "tracks," or infections on the back of the hand or the forearm, or abcesses on the thigh or arm may betray injections of various substances. A brown discoloration between the thumb and index finger is caused by holding a "joint," in contrast to the discoloration between index and middle fingers that comes from cigarettes. A rash around the nose and mouth could be from solvent sniffing. Solvents also cause inflammation of the eyes. Marihuana and alcohol may produce "red eye." "Snorters" of cocaine sometimes have a sore or ulcer of the nose membrane. A number of drugs cause dry mouth and lips. The sedatives and narcotics can produce sleeping in school and at unusual hours at home. Overactivity, restlessness, and impulsive behavior are more often associated with amphetaminelike drugs.

Chapter 12

The Drug Dilemmas

Many disconcerting dilemmas confront us. Some are practical, and they will be dealt with elsewhere in the book. Others are philosophic quandaries that the current drug scene provokes. Unless we acquire a philosophic base, our practical solutions will necessarily be superficial. They become patches that we slap onto the latest drug blowout. What seems needed is a long-range strategy that will provide a more sustained response to the issues that underlie drug abuse. To establish a philosophic posture is not an esoteric exercise. It is a necessary guide to understanding causes and designing treatments. Some of the drug dilemmas that always come forth in serious discussions are considered here in the form of frequently asked questions.

1 *Why can't I take whatever drug I please so long as no one else is harmed by it?*

We should have the basic right to do what we please with our body and mind. It is the latter part of the question that is perplexing. Is it possible to take drugs without the act impacting on others? Many drugs alter behavior and can result in disability. Others will be affected by that behavior and its resulting disability; those closest to us first, but conceivably anyone. We should strive for a balance between personal freedom and social responsibility. In a complex society social responsibilities intrude on our freedom and necessarily limit our ability to do whatever we want.

2 *Why have we seen an upsurge of drug abuse during the past 15 years?*

There are many causes: the synthesis of new compounds (LSD, etc.), the ease of transporting these chemicals anywhere (alcohol, barbiturates), the degree of social frustration, the attenuation of sustaining faiths in religion, country, and family, the many technological revolutions that are under way, the goallessness of both extreme affluence and extreme poverty. These are only some of the factors. It is possible that drug taking is also encouraged by our so-called drug-oriented society. Certainly, role models for the misuse of drugs influence children to move in that direction. Learning by copying the behavior of others may occur within the family or the school, or on the street.

3 *What is wrong with taking a drug to deal with a personal problem?*

Nothing is wrong—if it works. It works during the period of drug activity, but later the problem is back, made worse by the delay in solving it. When life problems are evaded, the technique for dealing with them in the future remains unlearned. Dissolving a problem with a chemical doesn't seem to work as well as resolving it through learning how to handle it.

4 *How can drug abuse be prevented? If everyone knew the facts wouldn't that solve the problem?*

It is not accurate to assume that teaching the facts will necessarily change a person's actions. There are many smokers, for example, who are convinced that cigarettes are bad for them, yet they continue to smoke. The best information is necessary, but attitudes and behaviors are only partly based on logic and reason. Emotional factors and conditioning are more important in making decisions about drugs.

5 *What should be done about marihuana?*

The dilemma here is that the legal penalties are usually more harmful than the harm from occasional use. From a public health standpoint this should not be. Punishment should fit the crime. From our current level of information, the decriminalization (not the legalization of marihuana use and simple possession) is a reasonable step.

Before legalization, it would be well to know some of the still unan-
swered questions about its long-term effects. The argument that we
have harmful drugs like tobacco and alcohol in the culture, so "Why
not pot?" is specious. Our two socially acceptable recreational drugs
were introduced at times when informed decisions could not be made.
Society has paid an enormous price for these mistakes.

6 *What is the significance of the psychedelic state? Is it a new
reality, a religious experience, or is it a chemical trick on the brain?*

It can be all of these and many other things. I have seen people
who have had a valuable and sustaining LSD experience that changed their
approach to life in the years that followed. I have seen others who have
been crushed by their exposure to a psychedelic, and have remained
psychotic for years. The great majority remained essentially unchanged.
The LSD experience is an enormous event for those who can integrate
it into their subsequent existence, but those who are unprepared may
be fragmented by it. And the majority remain unaffected.

7 *If intravenous amphetamines and cocaine produce such tre-
mendous highs. why not enjoy them?*

The central nervous system has a biphasic rhythm to its activity.
Waking is followed by sleep, excitation by depression, highs by lows.
The low that follows the stimulant high may be just as intense and
last a lot longer. What is more, the costs of amphetamine dependence
are a high price to pay for the stimulant rush.

8 *Why shouldn't anyone who wants to shoot heroin be able to
use it legally?*

Society has the right and duty to interdict certain behaviors that
are harmful to its members. Since heroin dependence is harmful, its
prohibition is a legitimate action. When all human beings are mature,
they will be able to make such decisions for themselves. Unfortunately,
we have not yet achieved maturity and wisdom. Our freedom is
encroached upon, it is true. but how much greater is the loss of
freedom of the addicted person?

A PARTIAL SOLUTION

Some suggestions are offered to those involved directly or indirectly in
the abuse of drugs. They are offered tentatively because no cookbook
recipe will resolve all issues and problems.

The Parents

One of the great myths of the day is that if a child goes wrong, becomes a head, for example, this must be due to parental failure. If the cause is not deprivation or neglect, it must be overprotection or possessiveness. At times it appears that the line between insufficient mothering and maternal smothering is nonexistent. This peculiar notion stems from the strong lay and professional indoctrination with the Freudian tenet that what happens in infancy determines subsequent behavior. Parents uncritically accept this thesis, and of course their children are quite willing to appropriate and elaborate on the theme that they received either too much or too little family love.

Unquestionably, substantial numbers of children are maltreated, abused, overcontrolled, or spoiled. This does not mean that they are completely incapable of overcoming these childhood handicaps. It would be both harmful and incorrect to believe that maladaptive personality patterns cannot be corrected. The individual has some responsibility in such matters. In addition, a large group of quite well-brought-up, characterologically sound children are "turned on" to drugs by their associates. It is difficult to discern how a parent can be blamed for these events. Sometimes, the parents are in a double bind. If they try to intervene, they are domineering; if they do not, they are neglectful.

Somewhere between "I don't care" and overprotection is the parental attitude that best permits children to develop and grow up. The child grows by solving problems, by learning from failure and defeat as well as from success and reward. The opportunity to become resilient by encountering and coping should not be denied any growing creature. When help is needed, the parent-child relationship ought to be so open and trusting that it is used for assistance, information, and advice. This is just as true for the issue of drug taking as for every other problem. Naturally, it would be best if drug usage could be discussed before the event, but the youngster should feel capable of talking about it afterward without fear of excessive emotionality or rejection. An open attitude need not mean acceptance of an act which the parent considers harmful. Approval is withheld, but condemnation should not be on an irrational basis. Sufficient data are at hand to point out quietly the personal, legal, and social hazards. Most often a single experience with drugs represents nothing more than the exploratory behavior of youth. If drug taking becomes habitual, it usually represents either a gratification that the young person should have been able to derive from daily living, or an evasion of life experience due to inability or unwillingness to meet life's day-to-day rebuffs.

Those most attracted to drugs are those who are bored, cannot enjoy, or cannot tolerate stress and frustration. The drug fits their emotional discontent and removes the necessity to plan, to struggle, to endure. In other words, the drug abuser was usually made long before the drug appeared. Drug dependence serves to compound the individual's problem with immaturity.

Parents who drink to excess will have an impossible task in persuading their sons or daughters to desist from drug usage. It is true that the parent's act is legal, and the child's is not. Nevertheless, the legality of alcoholic intoxication is not a strong argument to a child— or anyone else. Indeed, it sets an example of escapism that may be imitated.

Harsh and punitive attitudes make some children compliant, but many others rebel and become more involved in drugs as an act of defiance. Making obviously untrue statements about drugs is worse than useless. The child will tune out those who are patently trying to frighten him into desisting.

A difficult situation occurs when the young person is part of a group of drug users. Its members reinforce each other's drug taking. They become "authorities" and can outtalk parents. They may go on for some time before anything untoward happens. In such an instance the parent can hardly expect the child to abstain unless their relationship has been an unusually good one. What is more likely is that a critical moment will arise when the parent can step in and effectively help the child to stop using drugs. This moment occurs when someone in the group is hurt, someone is arrested, or someone else in the group decides to break away from the drug scene for philosophic or personal reasons.

Parents have a final responsibility which they cannot delegate to the school, the court, or the psychotherapist. However, they may have such feelings of guilt (sometimes unjustified) when their child becomes a head that they continue to support their offspring's deviant way of life. The parent is not necessarily guilty for a youngster's character deficit. Other people and circumstances have had powerful impacts on the child's character formation, too. It does not seem logical to underwrite an undesirable drug habit. Rather. the attitude should be, "I love you and I will help you, but I won't support you if you persist in behavior which I believe to be detrimental to you." Now that every large city has its counterculture heaven, this question comes up often. Regularly, parents who deplore the fact that their child has become a head, has dropped out of school, and has moved off to a counterculture ghetto perpetuate this sort of existence by sending the child money. Often funds from one parent will support a roomful of young people. This is unfair not only to the other youngsters but also to their parents.

Should a parent ever report a child's illegal behavior to the police or commit the youngster for mental hospitalization? This question can only be answered on a highly individual basis. If the youngster is involved with physically addictive drugs and will not voluntarily seek help, it may become necessary to take over the decision-making responsibility. If one's offspring has become a pusher, it may be justifiable to notify the authorities. Certainly, if the child has broken with reality and has no insight into his or her condition, commitment to a hospital may be the only proper step. Much depends upon the age; in the case of a minor, the parental responsibility is greater.

Most of the arguments that youngsters use to justify their bedrugged episodes are specious. Others are partially true, and a few are valid. If you, as a parent, set a poor example—have superficial and irrelevant goals and live according to irresponsible or inane standards—how can you hope to influence your child? The most convincing statement that can be made is your way of living. Striving for security, so important in times of hardship and poverty, is an inadequate goal during periods of relative affluence. Those of our middle-class children who do not need to struggle to obtain food and shelter find such an outmoded aspiration unacceptable. Beyond physical survival are more profound and appealing ideals. These should be sought and, by example, transmitted to our children. It is a feeling of existential meaninglessness that attracts some young people to the drug state. The acquisition of a sense of meaningfulness is the antidote. The current problem can be seen as a disease of affluence and nondirection. Many of this generation have not found ways and means of constructively using the time formerly expended on work to evade hunger. Freedom from want has produced a vacuum of time, which must be filled with meaningful activities, not time-consuming activities.

Sometimes a young "dropout" wants to drop back in after a year or two of the drug game. The family relationship ought not to be so embittered that he cannot ask for help to find his way back. A line of communication should be available to him. Sometimes a youngster wants to come back and return to school. She will have real difficulty admitting this to herself, her friends, and her parents. At this point, the real meaning of mature love can be made clear. Taking a child back without rancor or reproof will be an opportunity for a new beginning.

The School

It seems reasonable to insist that usage or trafficking of any illegal drug not be permitted on school grounds. Furthermore, psychological dependence upon mind-altering psychedelics, stimulants, sedatives, and intoxicants is contrary to the goals of the educative process, whether excessive use be on or off campus. If a place of learning is where one's intelligence, capabilities, and skills are developed and enhanced, then habitual displacement of consciousness, reality testing, and reasoning ability is antithetical to its goals. The frequent use of any drug can result in impaired performance. Indeed, a single use of some classes of drugs is associated with a temporary decrement in psychomotor functioning. Of all drug users, only those who indulge in the psychedelics claim consciousness expansion. From the observations of many who have studied this issue and from the reports of many who have gone the psychedelic route for years, chemical consciousness expansion is, for the majority, a myth. The revelations and enlightenments are all too often illusory. Occasionally, a valid insight may come forth, but it must be rigidly scrutinized during the sober state in order to determine its authenticity. Unfortunately, this is rarely done. Many who have acted upon psychedelic insights uncritically have met catastrophe.

If the educator is to learn anything from the current striving for drug-induced perceptual, emotional, and cognitive changes, it is that important areas of human experience have been neglected by our child-rearing and child-teaching practices. Many of those attracted to the drug experience suffer from *anhedonism*, the inability to derive pleasure from ordinary existence, and *alienation*, the inability to find meaning within or outside oneself. These are serious deficits, and in a young person they lead to serious disorders of behavior or character. From childhood through adolescence we are failing (1) to provide goals appropriate to our times, (2) to train the emotions and the senses, and (3) to set limits. Therefore, goallessness, an inability to enjoy, and an attenuated sense of social responsibility predispose to chemical escape, chemical hedonism, and the search for chemical enlightenment.

Teachers, in addition to making the educative process as interesting, constructive, and alive as possible, can also have a great influence on the decision to take or continue to take drugs. They are often the confidants when parents are lacking or have failed to accept their role. The teacher may be the first to learn of, or notice, aberrant behavior due to drugs, and may be able to help his pupil by talking things over. Thus must not be a taboo topic.

In schools where the administration believes that no drug activity is present, there may be reluctance to rock the boat by opening up the subject. The likelihood, though, is that more drug activity is going on than comes to the awareness of the authorities. Furthermore, in users and nonusers alike, a brisk interest in the drug phenomenon is evident. Newspaper and magazine articles are read, rumors are transmitted, and considerable misinformation is exchanged. It would seem that offering to provide drug information is part of the educative process.

The teacher, as a more neutral person than the parent, can counsel or refer the student to a counselor. It is important to understand what the drug means to the student. The counselor may be able to provide better nondrug alternatives once he or she knows what the drug represents. A school counselor may form a discussion group of students involved in drugs. One or more students who have passed through their drug honeymoon and have come back are very helpful in such situations.

One element that must be emphasized in all discussions about drugs is that their use is stupid, not smart or "in." Regular users even of nonaddictive drugs are in a state of maturation arrest. Drugs "solve" their problems; they do not learn to solve problems and endure dissonance in their environment. Many drugs leave the student goofy, unable to function. This is hardly a smart way to exist. Drugs that are supposed to expand one's consciousness all too often fail to do so, especially if one is young and unprepared. The growing brain is more vulnerable to all chemical agents, and temporary, perhaps even sustained harm can result. Permanent harm to the brain cells after exposure to large amounts of psychedelics is a possibility that is now undergoing intense study.

It is in peer groups that drug taking spreads. The teacher may become aware that one or a few individuals are proselytizing. An epidemic may be prevented by quick action in such instances. School authorities should make the school area a difficult place to obtain or use drugs. It is too much to expect that school authorities can be responsible for activities off the campus.

The question of confidentiality rarely comes up, but it may. If a student approaches a teacher as a friend to discuss her drug problem, she must be warned about the teacher's duties in the matter. It is to be hoped that it will be possible to listen without disclosing, but school regulations may prevent this. Under such circumstances the student must be clearly told beforehand. A certified school psychologist or psychiatrist has the advantage of being able to keep patients' statements as privileged communications. Referral to such a person will safeguard the student.

A repertoire of disciplinary measures with some built-in flexibility is preferable to rigid, mandatory punishments. The campus supplier of LSD and opiates is not in the same category as the youngster who has been persuaded to try a "joint," and whose negligence has resulted in detection. Strangely enough, the penalties for both offenses are equal in some states—they are felonies. Unfortunately, school authorities may have no choice in the matter. They are often required to report every breach of discipline. It may be well to make students aware that a felony involves lifelong consequences beyond incarceration. This should not be done as a threat, but rather as part of setting forth the realistic here-and-now risks connected with the misuse of certain drugs.

The Therapist

All too often the psychotherapist is faced with a young patient who does not want to be treated but has been coerced into the office by anxious parents. Little can be done if the patient is not motivated to change. All too often he is at a phase of his drug-taking cycle when he is deriving satisfaction, euphoria, and release of tension from the chemical being used. He is feeling no pain; what can therapeutic intervention offer? The "illness" is pleasant, the cure much less so. If his drug happens to be one of the psychedelics, he has a feeling of subjective wisdom far beyond that of the therapist. He may have a pseudophilosophic jargon which can put many a therapist down. If such patients cannot somehow be motivated to examine themselves and their reasons for overusing drugs, little can be accomplished. They are unlikely to remain in treatment, and it is the parents who should be counseled about their attitudes at this point.

Sooner or later, after a few bad trips, a psychotic break, or disillusion with the drug way of life, the devotee will want out. Perhaps it is merely that she sees the circular, pointless nature of her existence. For though an agent like LSD may be helpful in directed psychotherapy, its undirected use all too rarely has a significant psychotherapeutic impact. At this moment the skilled therapist who knows something about the nature of the psychedelic experience can perform a valuable service. The drug practices of the past months or years must be carefully examined to learn as much as possible from them. Their meaning to the patient must be uncovered and understood. Thus a bridge is built that leads the patient back into an enjoyment of this world; a reentry into this life is provided in the best possible manner. These are the most difficult of patients to treat, for they are engulfed in the psychedelic life because of their unfulfilled needs. They have tasted great gratifications in their responsibility-free, hedonistic existence. Now the therapist must help them become more responsible, find more significant goals, and begin the long, hard process of psychological maturation. The immaturity which caused them to seek the magic pill must be modified. These are valuable people, often very bright and with many contributions to make. After a period of individual therapy, a psychotherapeutic group may be a place where the members can find the values of the human interaction.

The Legislator

The control of the drugs mentioned in this book is necessary especially, but not only, for the juvenile. Passing laws can have a beneficial or a harmful effect, depending upon the wisdom of the legislation. With the current upsurge of drug misuse, especially in those of school age, it would seem reasonable to apprehend the supplier of these minors rather than to focus on catching the juvenile user or possessor. The maker, the smuggler, the pusher, and the transporter must be found and punished. The penalties for use and possession of a drug like marihuana are excessive, and excessive punishments may defeat the legislative purpose. There is no logic in treating marihuana, a weak hallucinogen, like heroin.

The mere passage of laws as a device to eliminate noxious behavior is an ineffective technique. The hope that a decree will abolish undesirable conduct in a democratic society is just as naive as the expectation that a chemical potion will magically change character. In addition to sagacious laws, public education and public cooperation with the laws are needed. Somehow these must be obtained.

The User

The last words are for the student or ex-student who is overinvolved in some mind-altering drug. This will be no exhortation to desist; any genuine change must start with you. Instead, let's deal as simply as possible with some of the basic questions. One question you might ask is, "What's wrong with instant joy or chemical escape?" My own answer would be, "Nothing, if it works." The trouble is that from what I have seen, "joy for free" doesn't work. Tolerance to pleasure seems to develop just like tolerance to drugs. This is so well known that it forms the themes of innumerable novels and movies. Constant ecstasy becomes less and less ecstatic. It eventually crumbles into nothing. Synthetic happiness satisfies, then satiates, and chemical escape is for today. What of tomorrow? Tomorrow, you may need "louder music and stronger wine" in order to fly. Tomorrow, you may need something stronger than pot, speed in the acid, a switch to the exaltation that is cocaine or to the quiet rapture of heroin. The search for the ultimate euphoria is never ending. "Pleasure now, pay later" is fine until the bills start coming in. One young man who had been through it all said it very simply, "You've got to pay your dues." If payment is delayed too long, the amount becomes staggering.

"But I can't make it without drugs, I can't get way out there or enjoy," you will say. That is your inadequacy, your immaturity speaking. That is where you will stay if you lean on drugs. Everything that can be obtained with drugs can be accomplished without them. It

SUMMARY OF DRUG EFFECTS

Drugs	Legal status, manufacture, and sale	Legal status, possession, and usage	Withdrawal symptoms	Physical dependence	Death by overdose	Accident proneness during use	Suicide tendencies
LSD	Felony	Misdemeanor, various state laws	No	No	No	Yes	Yes
Marihuana	Felony	Violation, misdemeanor, or felony	No	No	No	Yes	Very rare
Heroin	Felony	Felony	Vomiting, diarrhea, tremors, aches, gooseflesh, sweats, etc.	Yes	Coma, respiratory failure, shock	Yes	Yes
Barbi-turates	Legal medically, felony for illegal sale	Misdemeanor, various state laws	Delirium, tremors, convulsions	Yes	Coma, respiratory failure, shock	Yes	Yes
Ampheta-mines	Felony for illegal sale	Misdemeanor, various state laws	Depression, apathy, muscle aches	Yes	Convul-sions, coma, cerebral hemorrhage	Yes	Yes
Cocaine	Felony	Felony	No	No	Convul-sions, respiratory failure	Yes	Yes
Airplane glue	No restrictions	None, or misdemeanor by city or state law	Mild	Rare	Asphyxia-tion, heart stoppage	Yes	Unknown
Alcohol	Various state laws for illegal stills	Sales to minors a misdemeanor; various state laws on driving, disorderly conduct	Delirium, other symptoms, tremors, convulsions	Yes	Coma, respiratory failure	Yes	Yes

Physical complications	Chromosomal changes	Mental complications during use	Mental complications after use	Tolerance	Manner used	Abuse trend
Rare	Questionable	Panic, paranoid states, anxiety	Amotivation?, flashbacks, psychoses, paranoia, anxiety reactions, brain damage	Extremely rapid	Orally, injection	Decreasing
Bronchitis, conjunctivitis	Questionable	Rare panic or paranoid states	Amotivation?, rare psychoses, rare, flashbacks	Yes	Orally, smoking	Increasing
Infections, hepatitis,	Reported	Coma	Asocial and antisocial reactions	Yes	Injection, snorting, least effective orally	Decreasing
Overdose	Unknown	Intoxication, acting-out behavior	Psychoses	Yes	Orally, injection	Increasing
Malnutrition, needle contamination	Unknown	Paranoid, assaultive	Paranoid psychoses, asocial reaction	Yes	Orally, injection, nasal and other membranes	Decreasing
Malnutrition, perforated nose septum from sniffing	Unknown	Excited state, intoxication	Probable brain damage, paranoid psychoses	Yes	Injection, nasal and other membranes	Increasing
Bone marrow depression, liver and kidney damage	Unknown	Excited state, intoxication	Brain damage?	Slight	Inhalation and sniffing	Stable
Gastritis, pancreatitis, cirrhosis, neuritis	Unknown	Intoxication acting-out behavior	Brain damage, psychotic reactions	Partial	Orally	Increasing

means work, development, growth. The rewards are infinitely greater because you will have done it yourself. You will have paid your dues first, and the joy will be so much more genuine because it will be a reward for something you have actually accomplished. Do you want release from tensions, a feeling of joy just from being alive? Do you want to empathize with people, be free and more spontaneous? Non-chemical ways are available, but they require training and discipline. Are you willing to pay that price?

Additional Reading

GENERAL

Blum, R. H.: *The Dream Sellers*, Jossey-Bass, San Francisco, 1972.

Brecher, E. M.: *Licit and Illicit Drugs*, Consumers Union, Mt. Vernon, New York, 1972.

DeRopp, R. S.: *Drugs and the Mind*, St. Martin's Press, New York, 1957.

The Drug Takers: Time-Life Special Report, Time, Inc., New York, 1965.

Drug Use in America: Problem in Perspective, Second Report of the National Commission on Marihuana and Drug Abuse, Washington, D.C., 1973.

Federal Strategy for Drug Abuse and Drug Traffic Prevention, Strategy Council on Drug Abuse, Washington, D.C., 1974.

Final Report of the Commission of Inquiry into the Non-Medical Use of Drugs, Information Canada, Ottawa, 1973.

Goodman, L. S. and A. Gilman: *The Pharmacologic Basis of Therapeutics*, 4th ed., Macmillan, New York, 1970.

Zarafontis, C. J. D. (ed.): *Drug Abuse: Proceedings of the International Conference*, Lea & Ferbiger, Philadelphia, 1972.

THE PSYCHEDELICS — LSD AND OTHERS

Aaronson, B. and Osmond, H.: *Psychedelics*, Anchor Books, Garden City, New York, 1970.
Abramson, H. A. (ed.): *The Use of LSD in Psychotherapy and Alcoholism*, Bobbs-Merrill, Indianapolis, 1967.
Alpert, R. S., S. Cohen, and L. Schiller: *LSD*, New American Library, New York, 1966.
Cohen, S.: *The Beyond Within: The LSD Story*, 2d ed., Atheneum, New York, 1967.
Efron, D. H. (ed.): *Psychotomimetic Drugs*, Raven Press, New York, 1970.
Huxley, A.: *The Doors of Perception*, Harper & Row, New York, 1954.
Levin, L.: *Phantastica, Narcotic & Stimulating Drugs*, E. P. Dutton, New York, 1964.
Masters, R. E. L. and J. Houston: *Varieties of Psychedelic Experience*, Holt, Rinehart & Winston, New York, 1966.

THE PSYCHEDELICS . . . MARIHUANA

Cannabis, Report by the Advisory Committee on Drug Dependence, Her Majesty's Stationary Office, London, 1968.
Grinspoon, L.: *Marihuana Reconsidered*, Harvard University Press, Cambridge, 1971.
Marihuana-Hashish Epidemic and Its Impact on U.S. Security, Hearings before the Subcommittee to Investigate the Administration of the Internal Security Act, Washington, D.C., 1974.
Marihuana and Health, Fourth Annual Report to the U.S. Congress, Washington, D.C., 1974.
Marihuana: A Signal of Misunderstanding, First Report of the National Commission on Marihuana and Drug Abuse, Washington, D.C., 1972.
Nahas, G. G.: *Marihuana: Deceptive Weed*, Raven Press, New York, 1973.
Solomon, D. (ed.): *The Marihuana Papers*, Bobbs-Merrill, Indianapolis, 1965.

THE NARCOTICS

Chein, I.: *The Road to H.: Narcotics, Delinquency and Social Policy*, Basic Books, New York, 1964.

Cortina, F. M.: *Stroke a Slain Warrior,* Columbia University Press, New York, 1900.

DeQuincey, T.: *Confessions of an English Opium Eater,* Three Sirens Press, New York, 1932.

Fiddle, S.: *Portraits from a Shooting Gallery,* Harper & Row, New York, 1967.

Lindesmith, A. R.: *The Addict and the Law,* Vantage, New York, 1965.

Smith, D. E. and G. R. Gay.: *It's So Good, Don't Even Try It Once: Heroin in Perspective,* Prentice-Hall, Englewood Cliffs, N.J., 1972.

Wakefield, D.: *The Addict,* Fawcett, New York, 1969.

Wilner, D. M. and G. G. Kassebaum: *Narcotics,* McGraw-Hill, New York, 1965.

Yablonsky, L.: *The Tunnel Back: Synanon,* Macmillan, New York, 1965.

THE SEDATIVES AND TRANQUILIZERS

Barbiturate Abuse in the United States, Hearings before the Subcommittee on Health, Washington, D.C., 1973.

Garattini, S., E. Mussini, and L. O. Randall: *The Benzodiazepines,* Raven Press, New York, 1973.

Methaqualone (Quaalude, Sopor) Traffic, Abuse & Regulation, Hearings before the Committee to Investigate Juvenile Delinquency, Washington, D.C., 1973.

Smith, D. E. and D. R. Wesson: *Uppers and Downers,* Prentice-Hall, Englewood Cliffs, N.J., 1973.

AMPHETAMINES, COCAINE, AND OTHER STIMULANTS

Amphetamine Legislation, Hearings before the Subcommittee to Investigate Juvenile Delinquency, Washington, D.C., 1971.

Costa, E. and S. Garattini: *International Symposium on Amphetamines and Related Compounds,* Raven Press, New York, 1970.

Diet Pill (Amphetamines) Traffic, Abuse and Regulations, Hearings before the Subcommittee to Investigate Juvenile Delinquency, Washington, D.C., 1972.

Ellinwood, E. H. and S. Cohen: *Current Concept on Amphetamine Abuse,* U.S. Government Printing Office, Washington, D.C., 1972.

Kalant, O. J.: *The Amphetamines: Toxicity and Addiction,* Charles C Thomas, Springfield, Illinois, 1966.

National Clearinghouse for Drug Abuse Information: *Cocaine*, Series 11, No. 1, 1972.

Sjoqvist, F. and M. Tottie: *Abuse of Central Stimulants*, Almqvist & Wiksell, Stockholm, 1969.

THE VOLATILE SOLVENTS AND OTHER ANESTHETICS

Cohen, S.: "The Volatile Solvents," *Public Health Reviews*, 2:185–214, 1973.

Conference Proceedings on the Inhalation of Glue Fumes and Other Substance Abuse Practices Among Adolescents, U.S. Government Printing Office, Washington, D.C., 1968.

National Clearinghouse for Drug Abuse Information: *The Deliberate Inhalation of Volatile Substances*, Report Series 30, No. 1, July 1974.

ALCOHOL, A DANGEROUS DRUG

Alcohol and Health, Second Special Report to the Congress, U.S. Government Printing Office, Washington, D.C., 1974.

Bacon, M. and M. B. Jones: *Teen-age Drinking*, Crowell, New York, 1968.

Cahn, S.: *The Treatment of Alcoholics: An Evaluation Study*, Oxford University Press, New York, 1970.

Kissen, B. and H. Begleiter: *The Biology of Alcoholism*, Plenum, New York, 1974.

Wallgren, H. and H. Barry: *The Actions of Alcohol*, Elsevier, New York, 1971.

DELIRIANTS, OLD AND NEW

Efron, D. H. (ed.): *Ethnopharmocologic Search for Psychoactive Drugs*, U.S. Public Health Service Publication, 1045, 1967.

Gowdy, J. M.: "Strammonium Intoxication," *J. Amer. Med. Assn.*, 221:585–589, 1972.

Puharich, A.: *The Sacred Mushroom*, Doubleday, Garden City, New York, 1959.

Wasson, R. G.: *Soma: Divine Mushroom of Immortality*, Harcourt Brace Jovanovich, New York, 1971.

THE "HEAD"

DeRopp, R. S.: *The Master Game: Beyond the Drug Experience*, Delacorte Press, New York, 1968.

Kalant, H. and O. J. Kalant: *Drugs, Society and Personal Choice*, General Publishing Company, Ontario, Canada, 1971.

Marin, P. and A. Y. Cohen: *Understanding Drug Use*, Harper & Row, New York, 1971.

National Clearinghouse for Drug Abuse Information: *Al'ernatives to Drug Abuse: Steps Toward Prevention*, Publication No. 14, Washington, D.C., 1973.

THE DRUG DILEMMAS

Blum, R. H.: *Horatio Alger's Children: The Role of the Family in the Origin and Prevention of Drug Risk*, Jossey-Bass, San Francisco, 1972.

Castenada, C.: *Journey to Ixthan: The Lessons of Don Juan*, Simon & Schuster, New York, 1972.

Snyder, S.: *Madness and the Bruin*, McGraw-Hill, New York, 1974.

Weil, A.: *The Natural Mind*, Houghton Mifflin, Boston, 1972.

Glossary
of Drug Slang

Acapulco gold High-grade marihuana

Acid Lysergic acid diethylamide, LSD

Acidhead Regular user of LSD or other hallucinogens

Amped High on amphetamines or other stimulants

Angel dust PCP, phencyclidine, Sernyl, Sernylan. Also known as "Hog" and the "Peace Pill." An animal tranquilizer-anesthetic with hallucinogenic effects.

Bag Packet of drugs; the category one fits into

Ball Sexual intercourse; absorption of stimulants placed in vagina

Barbs Barbiturates

Bennies Benzedrine, an amphetamine

Blank Extremely low-grade narcotics

Blast Strong effect from any drug

Blind munchies Craving to eat after smoking marihuana

Blue angels Amytal capsules, a barbiturate

Blue velvet Mixture of paregoric (camphorated tincture of opium and Pyribenzamine (an antihistamine) for intravenous injection

Bombita   Amphetamine injection sometimes with heroin added
Boot   Draw blood into the dropper in order to get all the heroin, then reinject it
Bummer   Bad trip with LSD or other drugs
Burn   Sell bad dope
Bust   An arrest
Cap   Capsule containing drugs
Carry   In possession of illicit drugs
Cartwheels   Amphetamine tablets scored crossways
Chipping   Taking heroin occasionally, for example, "weekend chipper"
Christmas trees   Dexamyl spansules, amphetamine and Amytal mixture
Cibas   Doriden, a nonbarbiturate sleeping pill
Clean   Not using drugs
Coasting   Feeling good after taking a drug
Coke   Cocaine
Cold turkey   Effects of sudden narcotic withdrawal (from the goose-flesh which resembles the skin of a cold, plucked turkey)
Coming down   Recovering from a drug trip
Connection   Person from whom one buys drugs
Contact high   Euphoria from being with people who are high from drugs
Cook up   Heat heroin and water in a spoon prior to injection
Cooker   Bottle top for heating the heroin and water
Cop   Make a buy of heroin
Cotton   Cotton used to strain a fix of heroin before injection
Crank   Methedrine with impurities
Crash   Sudden withdrawal from amphetamines
Crash pad   Place to come down from a drug or to spend a night
Crystal   Methedrine powder
Crystal palace   Place where speedfreaks go to inject
Cut   Dilute drugs by adding inactive substances
Deal   Sell drugs
Deck   Number of drug packets
Dexies   Dexedrine, an amphetamine
Dime bag $10 package of heroin
Dirty   Possessing drugs, liable to arrest if searched
Dollies   Dolophine, trade name for methadone
Dope   Originally heroin, now any illicit drug
Doper   Person who uses drugs
Downer   Any sedative, tranquilizer, narcotic, or alcohol
Drop   Swallow a drug
Dummy   Purchase that contains no narcotics

Dynamite   Very good heroin
Eighth   Eighth of an ounce of heroin, two spoons
Elephant   PCP, Sernyl
Fix   Injection of narcotics
Flash   High as after a cocaine injection
Flashback   Recurrence of a psychedelic experience without drugs
Flip out   Become psychotic
Floating   In a drug-induced reverie
Fluff   Make a drug bulkier by pulverizing it or adding an adulterant
     like talc
Footballs   Oval-shaped amphetamine tablets
Freak out   Lose control or become psychotic under drugs
Garbage   Poor-quality heroin
Get down   Inject heroin
Get off   Take or feel the effects of a drug
Girl   Cocaine
Goofballs   Sleeping pills
Grass   Marihuana
H   Heroin
Hard stuff   Narcotic, usually heroin
Hash   Hashish, the resin from cannabis
Head   Heavy user of drugs
Hearts   Dexedrine tablets (from the shape)
Heat   The police, also "fuzz," "narcs," or "the Man"
High   Euphoria, usually from drugs
Hit   Shot of dope
Hog   PCP, Sernyl
Holding   Having drugs in one's possession
Hooked   Addicted, physically dependent
Hophead   Narcotics addict
Horse   Heroin
Hot shot   Bag of pure heroin or one that has been deliberately poisoned
     to kill an informer or undercover man
Hustle   Obtain money or merchandise other than by working for it
Hype   Narcotics addict
Joint   Marihuana cigarette, also jail
Jolly beans   Pep pills
Jones   Physically dependent on heroin
Joy-pop   Inject heroin irregularly
Juice   Whiskey
Junkie   Heroin addict
Key   Kilogram

Kick   Stop using heroin (from the muscle jerks)

King Kong   Very large heroin habit (from monkey on your back)

Layout   Equipment for intravenous injections

Leapers   Amphetamines

Lemonade   Weak bag of heroin

Lid   Ounce of marihuana (from metal tobacco cans in which it was once sold)

Loaded   Very drunk on a drug

Looking   Seeking a pusher

Luding out   Getting drunk on Quaalude and alcohol

M   Morphine

Mainline   Inject drugs into a vein

Maintaining   Keeping at a certain level of drug effect

Manicure   Removing the dirt, seeds, and stems from marihuana

Mellow yellow   Brand of banana peel, without any effect

Mesc   Mescaline

Meth   Methedrine, speed

Mike   Microgram (of LSD), millionth of a gram

Miss   Inject a drug outside a vein accidentally

Munchies   Desire to eat sweets while smoking marihuana

Needle freak   Someone who gets pleasure out of injecting water or weak drugs

Nickel bag $5 bag of heroin

Nixon   Low-quality drugs

Nod   Doze after heroin or methadone

Nod out   Sleepy state after narcotic use

O. D.   Overdose of narcotics or other downers

Outfit   Apparatus for injecting heroin, usually an eyedropper and needle

Overamped   Poisoned by an overdose of amphetamines

Panama red   Good grade of marihuana

Panic   Shortage of heroin on the street

Pillhead   Heavy user of uppers or downers or both together

Pipe   Large vein easy to hit

Poppers   Amyl nitrite ampules

Pothead   Heavy user of marihuana

Purple hearts   Dexamyl. a combination of Dexedrine and Amytal (from the shape and color)

Purple Owsley   LSD

Pusher   Lowest level of drug dealer

Quarter $25 bag of narcotics

Quill   Matchbook cover for sniffing cocaine or heroin

Rainbows Tuinal (Amytal and Seconal), a barbiturate capsule in a red and blue capsule

Reds Seconal, a barbiturate, also Mexican reds, a smaller-sized sleeping capsule

Reentry Coming down from a psychedelic trip

Righteous High quality

Rip off Steal or deceive

Roach Marihuana butt

Roach holder Device to hold the roach so that it can be smoked down to the end

Run Take amphetamines for a number of days

Rush Ecstatic moment after injecting cocaine or amphetamines

Satch cotton Cotton used to strain heroin solution before injecting, often used after supplies run out

Scag Heroin

Score Obtain drugs

Shit Heroin

Shoot up Inject drugs

Shooting gallery Place where people inject drugs

Skin popping Injecting heroin under the skin

Sleeper Sleeping pill

Smack Heroin

Smeck Heroin

Smoke Wood alcohol

Snitch Informer

Snorting Sniffing or inhaling drugs like cocaine

Snowbird Cocaine user

Soaper Quaalude, Sopors, a sleeping pill

Spaced out Mentally disorganized from a drug

Speed Methedrine, an amphetamine

Speedball Injection of a stimulant and a depressant, usually heroin and cocaine

Speedfreak Heavy user of amphetamines

Spike Hypodermic needle

Splash Amphetamines

Spoon Measure of drugs, about one or two grams

Stash Supply of drugs in a secure place

Stick Marihuana cigarette

Stoned Intoxicated from some drug

Stoolie Informer

Straight Someone not on illicit drugs, a square

Strawberry flats LSD

Strung out   Addicted
Stumblers   Downers
Sunshine   Orange-colored tablets of LSD
Tab   Tablet, or "shoot up"
Take off   "Drop" a drug
Tie off   Put a tourniquet on a vein prior to injecting
Toke   One puff on a joint
Tracks   Scars and discoloration along a skin vein after many injections
Trip   Drug experience, usually with a psychedelic
Turn on   Take or give a drug
Turps   Elixir or Terpin Hydrate with Codeine, a cough mixture
Uppers   Stimulants
Using   On a drug
Wallbanger   Rowdy, intoxicated individual
Weed   Marihuana
Wiped out   Intoxicated
Wired   Addicted to stimulants
Works   Equipment for injecting drugs
Yellow jacket   Nembutal, a barbiturate
Yen sleep   Drowsy nightmarish period during heroin withdrawal
Zonked out   Comatose, intoxicated